HOMETOWN HEROES

Stories and Insights from
World War II Veterans
from Southeast Colorado

Compiled by
Donna McDonnall

HERITAGE BOOKS
2007

HERITAGE BOOKS
AN IMPRINT OF HERITAGE BOOKS, INC.

Books, CDs, and more—Worldwide

For our listing of thousands of titles see our website
at
www.HeritageBooks.com

Published 2007 by
HERITAGE BOOKS, INC.
Publishing Division
65 East Main Street
Westminster, Maryland 21157-5026

Copyright © 2006 Donna McDonnall

Stories and photos by Donna McDonnall
Military photos courtesy of the veterans

All rights reserved. No part of this book may be reproduced or transmitted in any form or by any means, electronic or mechanical, including photocopying, recording or by any information storage and retrieval system without written permission from the author, except for the inclusion of brief quotations in a review.

International Standard Book Number: 978-0-7884-3837-0

This book is dedicated to:

The memory of our son, David McDonnall,
killed in Iraq, 2004

My brother, Don Treffer, who served in
the U.S. Army in Germany during the 1960's

and with

Admiration and Appreciation,
to the courageous men and women
serving our nation
in the past, present, and future

TABLE OF CONTENTS

Lyle Brown	1
Kenneth Siegman	7
James Gourley	11
Scott Tidswell	17
Barney Miller	21
Clyde Kennedy	23
Henry Andersen	27
Milford Rasmussen	31
Alfred Darbyshire	35
Donald Wagner	39
Elmer Sniff	43
Thomas Sandoval	47
Nick and Lawrence Saldana	51
LeRoy Nickelson	53
Laurencio Via	57
Jewell Seufer	59
Darrell Seufer	63
Howard Ragsdale	67
Harold Smith	69
Fern Morgan	71
Robert Sanderson	73
Jack Hall	77
Ray Estrada	81
Henry Leal	85
Cliff DePree	87
Bob Lubbers	91
George Frank	97
James Hanagan	99
Willy Bridge	103
Howard Herbaugh	107
George Allen	111
History of Veterans Day	115
Background of Memorial Day	117
Prowers County Veterans Memorial	121

ACKNOWLEDGMENTS

I gathered the material for the stories in this book from personal interviews with the veterans. The information for the history of Veterans Day and Memorial Day was obtained from various internet websites, including the Veterans Association website and the U.S. Embassy websites. Thank you to Carol Grauberger for furnishing the memorial information about the Prowers County veterans who died in each war.

Thank you to the *Lamar Daily News* for inviting me to interview these veterans and sharing their stories in their "Salute to Veterans" monthly column.

Thank you to my husband, Bruce, for accompanying me on many of the interviews and helping me understand the situations and equipment the veterans described. Thank you, also, for encouraging me to compile these stories into a book and exercising much loving patience during the process of putting it together.

Thank you to our children and their spouses: the late David McDonnall and his wife Niki; Danny; Sara, and her husband Michael. You have always offered support and given me words of encouragement along the way. You also helped me through the nuts and bolts (or computers and cameras) of modern technology.

Thank you to our friends and family for proofreading this manuscript, giving counsel, and encouraging me. Without you, this book would still be a pile of stories in my file drawer.

Most importantly, thank you to all the veterans for inviting me into your homes and sharing your stories with me. Thank you to all the veterans who have served our country during times of war and peace. Thank you to those still in the service of our country.

You are all our hometown heroes.

INTRODUCTION

For almost three years, I interviewed World War II veterans living in Prowers County, a rural county in Southeast Colorado. It was one of the most rewarding and interesting experiences of my life. Their stories were funny, sad, courageous, and human, but always amazing. This book contains their stories and the insights gleaned from the veterans' experiences. Some of these stories appeared in *The Lamar Daily News* in their "Salute to Veterans" monthly column.

Their stories represent the wartime experiences shared by generations of veterans from across our nation. Veterans who have fought in the theaters of Europe, the savannahs of Africa, the islands of the South Pacific, the winters of Korea, the jungles of Southeast Asia, and even today, in the sands of the Middle East.

This is not a complete listing of all the World War II veterans living in Prowers County. I pursued several methods of finding all these veterans. Some I never discovered. Some declined interviews. I extend my respect and appreciation to all.

My purpose in compiling these stories is to honor those who served and to give the rest of us a deeper appreciation for what they endured.

Lyle Brown Walks Many Miles in One Pair of Boots

"I've been one of the luckiest guys there are. I've had my ups and downs, but overall, I've been mighty lucky," stated Lyle Brown detailing his service as a flight engineer during World War II.

Working in a California mining company, Lyle returned home December 7, 1941 to hear his wife, Norma, ask, "Did you hear on the radio the Japanese have bombed Pearl Harbor?"

Lyle didn't wait to serve his country. "My younger brother was in the Air Force at the time, so I decided to get into the flying side of things as well."

He moved his wife and five-year-old daughter to Arkansas to begin civilian training in the Reserves. He was selected to be a flight engineer. As such, Lyle had to learn to operate all positions in the B24 bomber. "You had to be alert at all times, and sometimes 'alert' wasn't good enough."

After more stateside assignments, Lyle's crew made a stop in Brazil. "One night I stayed with the plane while the guys went into town. They returned with fancy black boots, chiding me for wearing my combat boots. 'I'm going to stick with these GI boots.'

Later, as the crew waited under the plane's wing during a driving rain, the paper insoles on those fancy boots started coming out. I was thankful for my old boots."

After bouncing around North Africa, Lyle's crew first became operational on April 30, 1944 with the 15th Air Force, 454 Bomber Group, 738 Bomber Squadron out of Cerignola, Italy.

"Our day started at 3 a.m. for breakfast followed by a briefing to find out where we were going that day. They had sick call before the briefing, because if you weren't sick before, you would be when you found out where you would be flying that day.

"There was a mechanic there who always griped that our flight crew had it easy. 'The mechanics do all the work while you guys just fly around a bit then come back and rest.'

"One day our gunner was sick, so the Colonel told the mechanic he was going to take his place." 'I'm no gunner,' the mechanic said.

'You are now,' the Colonel commanded. After that, we heard no more wise cracks about having it soft.

"It was a bit unnerving flying at 10,000 feet and hearing Axis Sally's crackly voice over the radio, 'Looks like the 738th is headed for such and such a place. Be prepared boys, we have folks there waiting for you.' They usually did, too.

"It was the 26th of June, on our 26th bombing run, on our bombardier's 26th birthday. We were on our way home from a raid on a refinery in Vienna when we lost both right engines. We were at 20,000 feet and losing altitude fast, when a couple fighter planes hit us.

"I watched as the seven crewmen bailed out. When I reached the cockpit, Thornton, the pilot, told me to jump. I remembered how they told us to jump, but let me tell you, doing it and telling it are completely different. I made two jumps that day, my first and my last. As soon as I pulled my D ring, I turned to see if the other two guys got out. All I saw was our aircraft going down and then a big explosion. I just knew they didn't get out.

"There were three Gerrys (Germans) waiting for me. They took me to a briefing station, searched me, stripped me, and then gave my pants back but no belt or shoes. Leading me downstairs, they shoved me into a black dungeon. It was then I heard a small voice from the corner, 'Take it easy, Brown.' It was Thornton! He had made it!

"It was Thornton's habit to wear two shirts and two pair of socks, which he quickly shared with me. When a guard showed up later, I asked for my boots back. Surprisingly, he gave them to me.

"I was taken to Stalag Luft IV, Compound A northeast of Berlin.

"During our imprisonment, the Germans moved us around from place to place in railroad cars. We would be so crowded in those cars that we couldn't sit down. It was standing room only. They'd put us up front near the engines because we had a large red cross painted on top of our car so the Allies wouldn't bomb us. The Allies would make runs at right angles to the train, just taking out the engine. We'd stop overnight. But the Germans had engines hidden away in the woods and would usually have the engine replaced by the next day, and we'd be up and running.

"When the Russians started coming in from the East, the Gerrys decided to move us prisoners north to Swienemunde. Three thousand of us started marching through the cold, rain and snow of February '45 wearing GI overcoats and stocking caps. We roped all of our belongings up in our GI blankets, which we carried on our backs. Sometimes it would rain so much and our wool overcoats would get so waterlogged and heavy, we'd have to carry them on our backs, rather than wear them.

"One night we stopped in an area with two barns. The Gerrys had a couple halftracks parked in the trees near there. We heard a recon (reconnaissance plane fly over). The Gerrys must have heard them too, because they moved their halftracks. Soon the GIs were bombing the heck out of the place because of those half-tracks. We couldn't blame them; they didn't know the Germans had moved them. Anyway, they hit one barn killing several prisoners inside. I was in the other barn, unharmed. I don't know why I was spared.

"My combat boots kept me going for the ninety days it took us to get there. When we arrived, we joined 4000 Battle of the Bulge prisoners.

"We were liberated by a group of Limeys (British soldiers) from Montgomery's outfit. We fought along the front line for two weeks.

"Wanting to get back to our old outfit, we started walking. After two or three days, we 'liberated' a German lorry (big truck) and started running down the borrow ditch against traffic. They never stopped us. I don't know how they knew what flavor we were; we were pretty grimy.

"We came to the Elbe River and a narrow pontoon bridge. 'I'm going to run this thing as far as I can,' I told the guys.

"It was rough going across that bridge, straight up one minute, down the next. But we made it.

"When we got to the other side, they sprayed us with DDT and issued us new clothes. But I kept my old boots.

"At Brussels, I had my first opportunity to wire my wife. It was May 17, our wedding anniversary, almost a year after I was taken prisoner of war.

"At Camp Lucky Strike in France, I ran into Thornton again. We saw Eisenhower there. Later, in England, I saw the Queen Mother. She looks much the same today, hasn't changed much in all these years.

"I crossed the Channel in a C46 and hitched a ride with a Navy convoy back across the Atlantic. I was discharged on October 24, 1945."

Lyle's wife had been living in Lamar, Colorado, with a sister-in-law during the war. Lyle settled in Lamar and opened a service station still wearing his old combat boots. He also worked for the county as buildings and grounds keeper.

Later, visiting Thornton in Kansas City, Lyle gave his boots to Thornton's friend who wanted war memorabilia.

He and Norma had another daughter. Both daughters married and live in Denver.

"Like I said, I've been one of the luckiest guys there are. Not everyone makes 26 bombing runs and lives to walk all the way back home in their same old combat boots."

Insight: "I remember how they told us to do it (jump from an airplaine). But, believe me, talking about something and doing it, are two different things."

POSTSCRIPT

Lyle Brown was finally awarded his POW medal at a ceremony at Lamar's Presbyterian Church some time after this article appeared in the Lamar Daily News. The medal was procured through the efforts of Congressman Bob Schaffer, with the assistance of Jace Ratzlaff in Schaffer's La Junta, Colorado, office and author, Donna McDonnall.

Colonel James R. Shumate, who was serving at Peterson Air Force Base in Colorado Springs at the time, came and presented Brown his long overdue medal.

Colonel Shumate challenged those present to think about the consequences if those men and women who served in World War II had not stepped forward. "Each generation," Shumate explained, " is faced with their unique challenges. They met their challenge willingly and courageously. We are called upon today to meet a similar challenge."

Kenneth Siegman, Ski Trooper, Credits Women for World War II Victory

Late in the year 1940, Kenneth Siegman received a letter from Franklin Delano Roosevelt, President of the United States of America. "Greetings: . . . you are hereby notified that you have now been selected for training and service in the Amy.

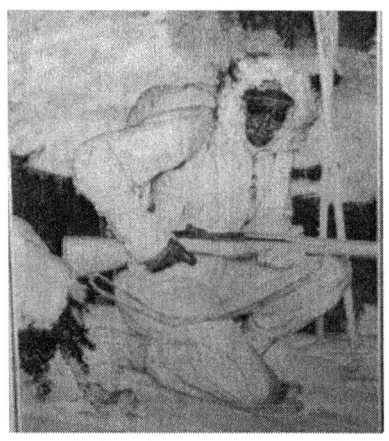

Siegman reported for his pre-induction physical on New Year's Eve 1940. After completing basic training at Ft. Ord, California, Siegman was ready to ship out to San Francisco as part of the 7th Division when he received his order to report to Elko, Nevada, and then on to Ft. Lewis, Washington. The 87th Mountain Infantry Battalion Reinforced was being organized on Mt. Rainier. This would later become the 10th Mountain Division. Troops soon arrived from such countries as Austria, Italy, and Norway.

The Eagle River Valley at the base of Tennessee Pass near Leadville, Colorado was selected as the construction site of Camp Hale, training grounds for the 10th Mountain Division. This location was ideal in terms of its natural features. The valley, situated at 9250 feet above sea level, was large and flat enough to accommodate the 15,000 soldiers to be trained there. The nearby rock cliffs and surrounding mountains provided the conditions needed to train the men in skiing, mountaineering, and cold weather survival.

In Nov. 1942, Siegman returned from Officer Candidate School in Georgia, to the newly completed Camp Hale. Camp Hale became the Cadre for the formation of the 85th and the 86th Infantry Regiments. By mid 1943, the Tenth Mountain Division was born.

It was the first and only mountain ski division in the United States Army.

"The training at Camp Hale was vicious. We spent two to three weeks in the mountains without benefit of shelter, fire, or hot food. Our sleeping bags were unbelievable however, and would protect us comfortably from the minus 45 degrees temperature we endured. The most important item of clothing was our clean, dry wool socks. At night we removed our ski boots, settled into our sleeping bag, laying on our back with a ski boot in each arm pit to keep them warm." If a ski boot was left outside, it would freeze immediately, and there would be no chance of getting it back on our foot.

The 10th Mountain Division was sent from the frigid heights of the Rocky Mountains to the sweltering heat of Camp Swift in Texas for a brief time.

In Nov. 1944, Siegman and the 10th Mountain Division were deployed to Italy. Company commander Siegman was promoted to Captain, and led B Company of the 86th Mountain Infantry Regiment. On Christmas Day they began the trek north to the Apennine Mountains.

The mission of the Division was to reclaim Mt. Belvedere from the Germans. To the southwest of Mt. Belvedere, ran a rugged line of snow-capped peaks, Riva Ridge. If Belvedere was to be taken and held, American forces must first secure this ridgeline, for it furnished an observation point for the Germans to watch every action of the American forces. As long as the enemy held the ridge, the movements of the Allied troops were limited.

During the predawn darkness of Feb. 19, 1945, B Company hiked up a jeep trail to the town of Pianacci. Their specific orders were to drive the enemy from the crest of Mount Capel Buso.

It was a rough five-hour climb. To understand the magnitude of the task before them, the men had only to look at the terrain. The ridge rose a seemingly insurmountable 1500 feet from the valley floor. Most of the trails were icy and rocky. Bending almost double under full field packs, the men scrambled up. One column had to use ropes. Slowly, but inexorably, they worked their way up.

In the blackness, B Company, the first unit to breach the German Gothic Line, moved in on the surprised Germans. The flashes of their rifles and machine guns outlined the top of the ridge, and the crackle of fire reverberated down the valley.

In an hour it was over. "Although we were subjected to two days of vicious counter attacks, we were able to cling to our objective," explained Siegman.

Recently, Siegman wrote a letter to the people of Pianacci: "Although I have thought of and still remember the kind people of Pianacci, I have been terribly remiss in not thanking them for their part in the successful completion of this mission. Had they not acted naturally (not alerting the Germans to the American presence), there was the distinct possibility that all of the men who climbed the mountain that night could have been blown from its side. Perhaps there are still inhabitants of Pianacci who remember this occurrence. To them and to all who now live there, I send my heart felt thanks and ask God's blessing for this wonderful mountain town. For as long as I live, I shall not forget."

Siegman received a reply from Pianacci, inviting him to return and visit their town.

For the next two months after driving the Germans from Mt. Belvedere, B Company fought several battles trying to clear the Po Valley. On April 25, they crossed the Po River in amphibious jeeps under artillery fire. A few days later, a German plane bombed the company causing heavy casualties, including 1 officer and 8 enlisted men. On May 2, 1945, they received word the Germans in Italy were ready for surrender.

At the end of the war in Italy, B Company was sent over Brenner Pass where Siegman received the surrender of the German troops.

From there, B Company moved to Bretto di Sotto on the Yugoslav border to thwart Marshall Tito's plan to take over. They were there for about three months.

The 10th Mountain Division was de-activated on Nov. 30, 1945.

Siegman spent some time in TX. training Puerto Rican troops before being sent to Berlin. His wife, Helen, and daughter, Karen, whom he hadn't seen until she was 18 months old, joined him in Berlin.

While in Berlin, he was sent to the Ski Championships in Garmisch, Germany. Competing against the pro-skiers of that day from all over the world, Siegman came in a respectable 13th in the Downhill and Slalom races.

Upon returning Stateside after his discharge in Nov. 1947, Siegman followed a friend to Granada, Colorado, where he worked for Holly Sugar and farmed for over 30 years.

During his retirement, he enjoyed watercolor painting, researching on the internet, and traveling with his wife.

Siegman fervently believed the war was won largely due to the efforts of the women who stayed on the homeland and worked in the shipyards, the aircraft factories, munitions plants, and war clothing factories. He also credits the women who volunteered for military service. He admonishes all of us to recognize the American World War II women, "to revere them, honor them, and cherish them. For, in reality, they preserved for you and me, a priceless gift-our freedom."

The 10th Mountain Division was re-activated in 1986. It has been deployed to Afghanistan in America's War on Terror. If the soldiers of today's 10th Mountain Division possess a fraction of the courage, valor, and physical prowess displayed by Major Kenneth Siegman and his men, Osama bin Laden is a dead man!

Insight: "Recognize the American World War II women, revere them, honor them, and cherish them. For, in reality, they preserved for you and me, a priceless gift-our freedom."

James Gourley Walks Through the Valley of the Shadow of Death

On March 16, 1942, when James Robert Gourley of Two Buttes, CO, entered the Armed Forces, his mother handed him a little pocket Bible. He carried that Bible in his pocket over his heart on every mission he flew. Little did he know he would literally walk through the valley of the shadow of death comforted by the words in that small Bible.

Gourley was stationed or landed at nineteen different air bases in the USA and abroad. He flew 48 combat missions, bombing 9 different countries (Romania, Poland, Germany, Austria, Czechoslovakia, Yugoslavia, Hungary, Greece, and Northern Italy), accumulating 216.5 combat hours, flying over ten countries, including one solo mission to Linz, Austria.

Born on a homestead in Texhoma, Oklahoma, Gourley graduated from Springfield High School, and later from Lamar Junior College and Amarillo Business College before joining the Army.

After being trained in several different capacities, Gourley arrived in Dalhart, TX, on April 6, 1944, where his crew was trained as a unit, Crew Zero 4, on B-17s. He flew as engineer while at Dalhart. Two weeks before they finished, he came down with the mumps and was quarantined. The rest of the crew left for Gulfport, MS. He arrived ten days later and learned he was reassigned as assistant engineer, radio operator, and lower ball turret gunner.

Gourley's B-17 crew. Gourley is front row, second from the right.

When Gourley's crew flew overseas, they were assigned to the 5th Wing in the 483rd Bomb Group Squadron. In this photo, Gourley is front row, second from right.

They flew their first mission Aug. 18, 1944. After they dropped their bombs and headed home, some German planes pursued them. Their tail gunner, Kitchen, shot a few rounds. The pilot asked, "Are the German planes that close?"

Kitchen replied, "No, but I wanted to make sure these damn guns work."

Jan. 21, 1945, Gourley was assigned to fly with a make-up crew to compensate for time he was hospitalized with leg injuries sustained in a tornado. After rousting out of bed at 4 a.m., Gourley dined on the typical breakfast of powdered eggs with half cooked bacon, burnt toast, and coffee that could walk. It was cold, dark, and raining. He went back to his tent for his usual candy bar, pack of gum and cigarettes, started to leave, and then returned and picked up more of the same.

Jim Pugh, his only tent mate asked, "What's the matter?"

"I'm not coming back," Gourley replied.

"Yes you will," Jim answered.

"Not today, Jim, but I need a favor, please. Pack my things in my duffle bag and take them down to headquarters if I'm not back in a couple of days."

With that, Gourley left to catch the truck to the flight line and helped the engineer check the plane over. "I don't want to fly today," the engineer said. "I don't feel right."

Gourley agreed, "I don't want to fly either."

When the colonel came, they explained their feelings. His reply, "Tuff shit! You are flying!"

Their plane encountered anti-aircraft fire enroute to their target, Nazi oil refineries in Vienna, Austria. When they crossed over the refineries, their bomb-bay doors were frozen shut. All their instruments were shot out. They had no communications of any kind. The other B-17s had dropped their bombs and headed home. Still loaded, Gourley's plane couldn't keep up with them.

After a few hours and lower altitude, they got rid of their bombs and belly-landed in a little field in about 3 or 4 feet of snow in Nazi-occupied territory near Banja Luca, Yugoslavia. None of the ten crew members sustained injuries. Before leaving the plane, they destroyed all the instruments so the Germans could not copy their technology.

They were quickly surrounded and taken away by Chetniks, a neutralist underground group. They were taken to the farmhouse of Dragutin and Vasilia Cvijanovic, along with two B-24 boys and an Italian.

Their sleeping quarters consisted of straw on the floor in one corner of the house, while the couple and their six children occupied the other bedroom and outside shed. Gourley had his parachute harness on with his GI boots tied to it when he went to sleep. The next morning, he awakened to discover someone had stolen his boots, leaving him with only his sheepskin flying boots.

The following day, they returned to their plane and burned it, per standing U.S. military orders.

The first couple days they tracked out SOS signs in the snow, hoping the bombers would see it. As planes flew over, they waved and hollered, but to no avail.

Mr. and Mrs. Cvijanovic and their children tried to help. The Germans had taken most of their food and livestock. Everyone hungered. Mrs. C. knew how to make the food stretch. At times they ate spoiled and fat meat, garlic, and dried field corn on the cob. The women did most of the work, while the men carried guns and kept patrol. Two of their sons, Milorad and Momchilo, told the GIs, "When we get big, we are coming to America to live just like you."

Two Chetnik guards watched them, not to keep them from escaping, but rather to protect them from the Germans. One night they were with several German prisoners in an old chicken house. At dawn, the guards took the German prisoners up in the mountains. Gourley's crew heard shots. After a time, the guards returned with no prisoners. Gourley wondered if they would be next.

They stayed with the Cvijanovics from Jan. 21 to March 12, 1945. Mr. C. called Gourley and his crew in and told them the Ustock (Yugoslav renegade young boys of 16 or 17 and Germans) were getting closer. Gourley's crew decided to make a break for it.

Gourley had a severe stomachache. Mr. C. gave him a water glass filled with 90 proof brandy and told him, "Bottoms up."

"It sure cured my stomachache," Gourley explained, "but I couldn't walk a straight line for quite some time."

Their group split up, with seven in Gourley's group and six in the other group. Walking through the mountains, they worked their way toward the front line where the Germans were fighting the partisans. They sent a scout out ahead. About mid-afternoon, they headed toward the town in the valley, marching in twos. As they marched through the town, there wasn't a soul on the street, but worried faces peered out behind curtains in every window.

They were about a hundred yards from a small hill, when a soldier in German uniform came over the hill from the other side. He yelled for them to halt. They halted. The Italian in their group yelled, "Americanos, Americanos."

After awhile, the soldier told them to advance. It turned out he was a partisan dressed in German clothing. He took them to a camp where they found a wagon filled with American shoes and clothing, but were given none of them.

The other group arrived the following day about noon. They had encountered gunfire from the renegade Yugoslavians, until the enemy's guns jammed, and they made their escape.

During their stay there, Gourley's group came under friendly fire from P-47s. Although a nearby bridge was completely destroyed, they escaped injury by diving in some brush.

On the 27th day, the partisans told Gourley's crew they would take them to an airport. They walked all day, but still no airport. Coming to a small village, they were told there was an American Embassy there. They were given K-rations. "Those K-rations tasted real good," Gourley explained.

The following day, Gourley and his group were put on British trucks and sent to Split, Yugoslavia on the Adriatic Sea coast. They boarded a fishing boat and sailed to the island of Vis. From there, they rode a captured German boat to Bari, Italy, on the other side of the sea. "It was a good feeling to get back and to have some GI food," Gourley described.

On March 30, they flew back to their old camp. "It really felt nice to touch down on the old runway once again." They flew to Naples, Italy and then onto Casablanca, and from there, to the U.S.A. in a C-54 without parachutes.

They landed at Washington National Air Base on April 21, 1945. The following morning they were interrogated by officers who threatened to make them pay for the B-17 they lost.

James Gourley was discharged Aug. 19, 1945 at Fort Logan, CO.

He returned to Baca County, CO, and later married Mary May Mackey on June 5, 1946. James returned to farming. They had five children: Sandra, deceased; Marcella (Swanson) of Walsh, CO; Robert Lynn of Two Buttes; Sherry Jo (Fisher) of Jefferson City, MO.; and Donna Mae (Crews) of Lawrence, KS. They have seven grandchildren and four great grandchildren.

James and Mary are active in the Two Buttes community. James still farms.

After his discharge, Gourley learned one of Mr. Cvijanovic's neighbors told the Germans about him helping the American flyers. The Germans captured and imprisoned him, beating him and breaking his kneecap. He lived with knee pain for over 30 years. His two sons, who had come to America as they vowed they would, brought him to New York, where he had surgery to replace his knee. He returned to Yugoslavia, where he now walks without cane or pain.

Those two boys also hosted a reunion for the flyers who stayed with them, combining it with the fiftieth wedding anniversary celebration for Mr. and Mrs. Cvijanovic. The crew remembered how they had walked 500-600 miles in the mountain valleys of Yugoslavia, facing imprisonment and/or death if captured by the Germans. James recalled walking every step with his mother's Bible in his pocket.

Insight: "A mother's Bible can help you walk through the valley of the shadow of death."

Scott Tidswell Endures As A Hero

When asked about his World War II experience, Scott Tidswell replied, "I'm no war hero. I just did what I was told." But as his story unfolds, he is a hero precisely because he did do what he was told.

Tidswell entered the military in July 1943. After basic training at Camp Roberts, California, he was assigned to a 81 mm mortar team with D Company, the 399th Infantry Regiment, 100th Infantry Division, with the 7th Army.

His unit was deployed to Europe in October 1944. They wintered near Marsailles near the Al Sace Lorraine Mountains between France and Germany.

During one of their major battles, the Battle of Bitche, the Germans attacked their unit on New Year's Day 1945. "We were in the Alsace-Lorraine region. Another unit that had been fighting with us pulled out. Before we could fill the gap they left, the Germans attacked. They broke through our lines and were shooting at us from the rear. I was in charge of loading mortar. When the order came to retreat, I was down in my hole cleaning my pistol with a toothbrush. We were instructed to leave our base plates, but take our mortar tubes. I quickly grabbed a can of corn beef hash and stashed it under my jacket. The next day, New Years Day, I retrieved that corn beef hash and had it for my lunch. That was certainly a memorable New Years dinner. Later, when we regained that territory, we went back and found our base plates."

They crossed the Rhine into Germany and engaged the Germans in the Battle of Heilbron. Soon the German troops began to dissolve. Victory was theirs.

For a while after that, Tidswell and his unit stayed in some of the smaller towns around Stutgart. Mostly they were involved with police action as the German troops withdrew.

During this time, he was busy with several activities. He helped organize a company school, which taught auto mechanics, welding, and other practical courses.

He also gave orientation lectures to a combat engineering group, doing much of his research in the Heidelberg libraries.

He helped other GIs find schools around Europe to attend. He took the opportunity to attend the London School of Economics.

Tidswell was discharged from the Army in April 1946 at the level of Staff Sargeant. Approximately 1000 men in his Division were killed, 3600 wounded, and 180 captured by the Germans.

Tidswell was asked to write the history of his Company in Europe. He published that book, "A Dog's (D Company) Life in ETO." He has corresponded with some of his old Army buddies through the years.

He also wrote about a battle he witnessed between a tank and a hydraulic "pill box." It was accepted for publication in the Smithsonian Magazine.

Tidswell was born in Garden City, Kansas, and attended the University of Kansas. He was later accepted at Stanford under the GI Bill, but he never attended.

Most hometown Lamarites remember him as the owner of Tidswell Furniture. "I was considered successful because we weren't forced out. Twenty-seven competitors came and went, but our store continued," Scott remarked.

His grandfather had started the business in 1912. His father helped in the store that was then the Adams & Tidswell Department Store. In 1946 his father bought out his grandfather, and Scott went to work there when he returned from the war.

"At first we sold about everything. But in 1952 we liquidated the dry goods and just went to home furnishings," he explained.

He retired in 1985, after 39 years.

His other accomplishments includes being on the First Federal Savings board for 32 years, an usher in the Methodist Church for over 40 years, active participation in the Elks and the American Legion.

He enjoys gardening, helping his sister-in-law who lives across the street, and telling middle school students about the war. He has several interesting artifacts he shows them.

Mostly he is proud of his wife, Luella, who he credits with raising successful children.

They had four children. Julie is married to Devlin Messmer, a newly commissioned officer in the Navy, stationed in Japan. Jennifer is married to Tom Munch, a musician in Pueblo, CO. She edits the Chronicle of Catholic Life. Their son, Jeff, is an optomitrist in Lamar, married to Cindy, the Lamar School Nurse.

Sadly, their daughter, June, died a couple years ago of ovarian cancer. They have five grandchildren.

Although Scott Tidswell is quick to give the credit to others, he is indeed a war hero, and an enduring hometown hero as well.

Insight. "Even a stashed can of corn beef hash is able to make a memorable New Year's meal."

Barney Miller Fights in the Battle of the Bulge

Barney Miller rushed through school, eager to get on with his life. He graduated from high school at 15 years of age and from North Texas State University at 19. "I wasn't pushed in school, I was shoved," he quipped.

He joined the Army June 4, 1943 and was sent to Mineral Wells, TX, for basic training. Then onto Camp Lee, Virginia, where he became part of a quartermaster corp. He was trained as a frontline psychologist.

Later, he was sent to truck driving school. "I couldn't even reach the pedals," he laughed. "The sargeant would just have to come by and throw me in the truck." Although his unit received a presidential citation, Miller was hoping to move on to a different branch of the military.

He applied to the Army Air Corps in Biloxi, Mississippi. However, he weighed twelve pounds short of the minimum. The officer in charge said if he could gain those pounds by 5 P.M. that day, he was in. "I ate bananas and whipped cream. I never want to see another banana!"

Miller was sent to Minnesota, but suffered appendicitis three days later. After recovering from his surgery, he found himself in the infantry, 385th Regiment of the 76th infantry division. The 76th had been wiped out during World War I, but the military reinstated it during World War II.

Miller fought in the Battle of the Bulge. "If it hadn't been for General Patton, we would have been wiped out," he explained. During the Bulge battle, Miller's feet froze.

His unit was the third unit into Germany. The first two units were turned back, so we were the first to establish a bridgehead.

In Germany, Miller's unit helped liberate four prisoner of war camps. "I have nightmares about the smell of rotting human flesh," he remembers.

Their unit had a printing press on a truck. They printed up leaflets warning the citizens of the towns they were approaching. "We advanced beyond some other units that way," he said.

When they were in the Marsailles wine valley in France, they had no water, only wine. He never did acquire a taste for powdered eggs reconstituted with wine.

He was discharged through San Antonio, TX.

After his discharge, he went to graduate school at Columbia University in New York. After two years in grad school, he went to Auburn University where he worked as an Associate Professor and helped develop the Department of Psychology.

He married his high school and college sweetheart, Beulah. His dad was his best man at their wedding.

After they were married, he put in a year at Ft Bliss in the reserves, serving in the Red Cross. The military wanted him to return to active duty, but he declined.

Barney and Beulah had three children. Their son, Terry, is in Alaska; Cheryn is in Thornton, CO; and John is in Flagstaff, Arizona. He has seven grandchildren.

Barney speaks of the current war with Iraq, "I can't even watch the news reports of all the killing. I have to go outside and tend to my flowers for awhile."

Indeed, driving by Barney Miller's home in the spring, one enjoys the view of a front yard covered in tulips. Today he is known as a gentle man who loves his flowers. But Barney can be proud of his military record and the courageous way he faced the horrors of war.

Insight: "Never hesitate to lend a helping hand."

Clyde Kennedy Finds Love in War

April 15, 1944, a young G.I. from Colorado spied a young lady across the dance floor in Wolverhampton, England. Leaning over, he whispered to a buddy, "See that pretty girl in the black dress over there. I think I will go ask her for a dance."

Thus began the courtship of Clyde Kennedy, Technical Sergeant with the 90th Infantry Division, and Marie Arrowsmith, a young British secretary. Their romance transcended agonizing months of World War II combat, long periods of separation forced upon them by the war, and departure from family and homeland to start life anew in a foreign country.

Kennedy graduated from the University of Colorado with a degree in Accounting and was employed in Cheyenne, Wyoming, when he was drafted into the Army in March 1942. Hoping to be assigned to Finance or Quartermaster, where he could use his college skills, he was counted off for assignment and sent to a Field Artillery Battalion with the 90th Division. They trained in Texas, the pine forests and swamps of Louisiana, and the deserts of California and Arizona.

Kennedy sailed from New York to England aboard the Queen Mary early in 1944. He was part of an Advance Party to set up camps in various parts of the English Midlands before the remainder of the division arrived. He helped set up camp for the Field Artillery at Worfield, named Camp Davenport. While they were at Camp Davenport, the troops could ride into Wolverhampton in the evenings and attend the dances at Civic Hall.

This budding romance started on the dance floor between an English lass and an American GI could easily have resulted in a mere passing pleasant memory for both of them. Only a month after their meeting, the 90th Infantry Division was ordered to vacate its various camps in the Midlands and move to the coast to ready itself for the Normandy invasion of France.

Kennedy was part of the invasion on Utah Beach. From there, "We saw Europe the slow way," he described. "Our division traveled down through France. As we were about to enter Germany, the orders came to move to the north to Belgium and Luxembourg to fight in what came to be known as the Battle of the Bulge." From there, they crossed the Rhine, continuing through Germany and into Czechoslovakia, when VE (Victory in Europe) Day came at last.

The 90th Division saw combat in five campaigns during 308 days of actual combat, more than any other division on the Western Front. The Division suffered approximately 21,000 casualties: with 17,000 wounded, injured or missing and 4,000 killed in action.

During World War I, the 90th Infantry was made up of men mainly from Texas and Oklahoma. Thus their shoulder patch was a red T/O. During World War II combat as part of the Third Army under the command of General Patton, the red T/O took on a new meaning. Patton called the Division his "Tough 'Ombres'," and the new name was used thereafter.

Kennedy was awarded the Bronze Star for heroic service in support of operations from June 19, 1944 to May 10, 1945. His commendation read, "Technical Sergeant Kennedy performed his administrative duties with efficiency and dispatch, often times working under intense artillery and mortar fire. On many occasions, he voluntarily accompanied his battalion commander on daring patrols through devastating fire of various calibers to assist him in reconnoitering forward areas."

Through it all, Kennedy and Marie continued their romance through correspondence with no knowledge of when they might see each other again. They have kept all these letters, over 400 in all, and treasure them to this day.

After victory in Europe, the 90th Division immediately began serving as part of the Army of Occupation. Two months later, Kennedy applied for a furlough to England. Marie had no idea when he was coming. One of Kennedy's buddies described their reunion, "Together again, Kennedy lifted Marie up and gave her a kiss and a big whirl."

Then one evening just before he left to rejoin his outfit, Kennedy asked Marie to marry him. He recalls, "She said 'Yes' in spite of not knowing when that might happen because the war with Japan was still on."

The 90th expected to be moved out of Europe for the invasion of Japan; however, that assignment ended when the atomic bomb dropped.

"The atomic bomb ended the war with Japan," Kennedy continued, "But the bomb I dropped when I wrote Marie I would be traveling to England to marry her, moved her and her entire family into stark reality, from 'what could happen in an indefinite future' into 'What do we do now?!!'"

On Sept. 26, 1945, they were married in England. After a quick honeymoon trip to Blackpool, Kennedy rejoined his division in Germany.

He returned to Colorado for discharge from the Army in December 1945.

He hoped Marie would soon join him. It was not until August, however, that Marie bid a farewell to her family, friends, and homeland and sailed across the sea with a shipload of GI brides to New York City. There she boarded a train for a long journey through Chicago toward the West.

Over fifty-seven years later, Kennedy reminisced, "We have returned to England fourteen times since then. Each time we return to Wolverhampton together, we make a special point of going to the Civic Hall where we met in 1944 and ask permission to go out on the dance floor to dance a few steps for old time's sake.

"A couple of times the hall was locked, and we were told by caretakers we could not get in. When they heard our story, however, the keys came from somewhere and, we'd be escorted onto the dance floor.

"When we walk in, I still see that pretty girl in the black dress and hear myself saying, 'I am going to ask that pretty girl for a dance.'"

Insight: "Love can be found even in the midst of war."

Lt. Henry Andersen Waits For His Discharge from the Navy

Entering a Nebraska post office back in Aug. 1941, Henry Andersen spotted a large poster of Uncle Sam holding a golden pair of wings. "What do these wings mean to you?" The poster questioned. Giving it some thought, Andersen decided those wings held a special attraction to him. He enlisted in the Naval Air Corp Reserves.

In Oct. 1941, Andersen was called to active duty and sent to Kansas City for flight training to what he calls "E Base- the E standing for 'eliminator.' You either made it or you were out. That wasn't wartime yet."

Riding a train Dec. 7, on his return from a weekend at home in Cozad, NE, Andersen heard the news of Pearl Harbor. He recalls spending Christmas that year guarding Lake Ponchatrain near New Orleans.

The following July, his heart called him back to Cozad to marry his childhood sweetheart, Marjorie Ford. Their mothers reported they first met when they were infants, less than a year old, at the Stitch and Chatter Sewing Club.

Following a short honeymoon trip, Andersen was sent to Floyd Bennet Field Naval Base in Brooklyn, NY. From July 1942 to the fall of 1943, he served as a ferry pilot, ferrying aircraft to the West Coast for the Pacific fleet.

Many times on the return, he would bring a fleet plane back. One such time he was flying a Navy Wildcat back, when he had to make an emergency landing in the Louisiana swamps. "I discovered one thing, those Navy Wildcats are not made to land in a cabbage patch. I ended upside down in that cabbage patch. Fortunately for me, a couple demonstrating true Southern hospitality dug me out. Then they invited me back to their house for some of that chicory coffee to calm my nerves. That stuff tasted like a bolt of lightening! They invited me to spend the night, but the Navy ordered me to Baton Rouge. I wish I could've gotten better acquainted with them."

Flying the return trip to NY, Andersen would land at La Guardia. He recalls watching workers dredge Jamaica Bay, building what is now JFK Airport.

During that period of time, the Navy employed civilian pilots as well as those trained in the military. This gave Andersen ample opportunity to meet some very interesting folks. Those that came to mind included, among others: a Texan rancher who knew Rosy the Riveter, Mary Pickford's husband, a stockbroker who knew people wherever they went, and the son of the man who coined the Phillip Morris ad.

Recalling life in the Navy, Andersen quipped, "There's the right way to do things, the wrong way, and then there's the Navy way."

Once I was ordered to fly a Navy Dive Bomber across country. "I told my commanding officer I didn't know how to fly it," Andersen explained. "He told me, 'You push the bar forward to go and pull back to stop.' I climbed in and reading the instruction manual, I flew that old clunker clear across the states. Made record time too. I caught a north-westerly wind current."

While her husband was stationed in NY, Marjorie lived on base on Long Island, surrounded by other military wives. They supported each other and helped them through periods of separation from their husbands. Everyone took care of everyone else.

She recalled one such incident when a GI took a woman to the hospital to have a baby. The woman's husband was away from home on assignment. An elevator operator, who was known to tip the bottle a little too much, asked, "Is this your first?"

To which the GI replied, "Nope, it's my second tonight." Rumors have it that elevator operator never touched a bottle again.

Andersen flew planes made by several different aircraft companies, such as Brewster, Grumman, and Vought-Sikorsky. He flew everything from single engine craft to those with four engines.

Andersen was sent to Hutchinson, KS, for his 4-engine training. Many years after the war ended, he and Marj returned to that base. "Everything was all gone. Weeds choked the runway. Nothing was there."

Andersen was never officially discharged from the Navy. He recalls Sept. 1945 when he was in Chicago. I was given orders to go back to where I came from and wait for further orders. "Well, I waited for over 50 years, when my son finally traced down my discharge papers."

In the meantime, when Andersen was returning to Cozad from Chicago, he stopped in Lincoln and enrolled in dental school at the University of Nebraska (UN), having taken his undergraduate studies at what is now the U.N. at Kearney. "That was on a Friday. They told me to start school on Monday."

After graduation from dental school, he was taking his licensing exams to practice in CO, thinking he might like to work in Longmont or Loveland. One of the examiners suggested he come to the Arkansas River Valley in Southeast Colorado.

Dr. Andersen practiced dentistry in Lamar from 1949 to 1983. "The people of Lamar are wonderful. They have treated us so well. I never want to leave."

He and Marjorie have two children, Sue, who was born in Brooklyn, and Ford, an attorney. They have two granddaughters and two great grandsons.

"Flying Ferry Command," Andersen said in summary, "was very interesting duty." He may humbly call it interesting work, but to those pilots and ground troops whose lives depended on a consistent supply of quality aircraft, it was vital.

Insight: "There's a right way to do things, a wrong way, and then there's the Navy way."

Milford "Bud" Rasmussen Sails on the Grey Ghost

Although born a Nebraskan, near Plainview, Milford "Bud" Rasmussen moved with his family to a farm near Stratton, CO, when he was very young.

He entered the service on April 7, 1942 and spent the six weeks of his basic training at Camp Robinson, near Little Rock, AR.

An aptitude test resulted in his placement as a munitions worker. He was sent to Barksdale Field near Shreveport, LA. There he became part of a four-section ordinance unit.

With twenty men to a section, this unit became part of the 319th Bomb Group assigned to the 437th, 438th, 439th, and 440th Bomb Squadrons.

Rasmussen's unit served a vital mission to the Army Air Corps: to deliver many different types and weights of munitions to the B-26 medium bombers. They also kept the machine guns on the planes in top-notch working order at all times.

Continuing training, his unit was sent to Harding Field, near Baton Rouge. After six weeks, the ground personnel boarded trains headed for Fort Dix, NJ. The troops rode barges out among several large troop ships and were directed to board the Queen Mary, known as the Grey Ghose during World War II. Rasmussen remembers the feeling of awe he experienced as they sailed past the Statue of Liberty.

This turned out to be one of the more notable crossings the Queen Mary made during the war.

Rasmussen was below deck in his cabin shaving on October 2, 1943, when he heard, "We hit it!" Since he hadn't felt any jarring motion or other disturbance, Rasmussen assumed the ship had struck a whale or other sea creature. Climbing topside, he was horrified to find the two halves of another vessel split apart and sinking fast in the wake of the Queen Mary.

Shortly before this time, the HMS Curacoa had been called up to serve as a protective escort for the Queen Mary. As was the habit, both ships followed a zigzag course in an effort to evade enemy fire. The Queen Mary steamed ahead at the speed of 28 knots, while the Curacoa traveled top speed of 26 knots.

Communications failed, and their zigzag pattern converged, resulting in the Queen Mary slicing through the Curacoa close to the stern. As the halves rapidly sank below the waves, only 101 of the 430 crewmen aboard survived.

With more than 11,000 troops on board, the Queen Mary could not take the chance of the enemy discovering she also sustained damage and sailed onward to Gurock, Scotland. Seventy tons of cement was used to temporarily patch the bow before it returned to the US for permanent repairs.

Rasmussen and the other troops on board the Queen Mary were given orders not to mention the incident. "I did not hear another word about this incident until the war was almost over. It appeared in the newspaper when I was stationed in Columbia, SC," Rasmussen recalls. Today photos of the accident are on display in the Queen Mary where it is moored in Longbeach, CA.

Rasmussen's unit then moved to North Africa, where they operated out of Morocco, Algeria, and Tunisia. From there, they served on Sardinia, off the coast of Italy, and onward to Corsica, off the coast of France.

During these operations, Rasmussen's ground unit received the Distinguished Unit Citation twice and the French Croix-do-Querre twice for performing their job with excellence, enabling the aircraft to carry out precision bombing maneuvers.

The 319th Bomb Group fought a total of nine battles.

Rasmussen returned to the United States in late January 1945 aboard the U.S.S. Westpoint.

During his thirty days R & R, Rasmussen married his teenage sweetheart, Valeta Seba. They had grown up on neighboring farms southwest of Stratton and corresponded while he was overseas. February 6th of this year (2002), they celebrated fifty-seven years together after walking down the aisle of the Stratton Lutheran Church.

After his discharge on October 15, 1945, Rasmussen

farmed for a year, then attended Barber College under the G. I. Bill. He and Valeta lived in Tribune, Bazine, and Hoisington, KS, as well as in Burlington, CO. In 1978 they moved to Lamar, where he owned his own barbershop on Elm Street for nine years.

They have five children: Mary Ann (Gary) Merritt of Ft. Lupton, CO; Deborah Montgomery of Lamar; Anita (John) Ackman of Colorado Springs, CO; Daniel Rasmussen of Lamar; and David Rasmussen of Sharon Springs, KS. They enjoy trying to "spoil" their nine grandchildren and ten great-grandchildren.

During his retirement, Rasmussen enjoyed working on their ranch and on the Wooten ranch.

When asked if it would bother him to sail on another ship, Rasmussen replied, "Not at all, I've sailed many times since the Queen Mary incident, and it has never bothered me."

Insight: "Sometimes you never know what hits you."

Alfred Darbyshire
Farm and Depression Era Helps POW Survive

July 12, 1944 Alfred Darbyshire, flying his 18th bombing mission as a waist gunner on a B24, heard the staccato "ack-ack" of the German anti-aircraft 88 artillery. Darbyshire's plane flew lead position just behind the radar decoy aircraft. They took a hit. One crew member was killed. The rest rode the plane down as it crashed near Munich, a short mile and a half from Switzerland. Immediately the German border guard captured the surviving nine crew members and transported them to Frankfurt for interrogation.

The Germans first imprisoned Darbyshire at Stalag Luft 4 with over 10,000 other POWs. He recalls one guard in particular, not-so-affectionately called "Big Stoop" by the POWs. "He would slap you or push you around whenever he felt like it. He had been taught treacherous techniques as a Hitler youth. The regular German draftees were pretty decent, for the most part," Darbyshire described.

When the Russians advanced closer to camp, the Germans moved the POWs on a forced march through bitterly cold weather to a POW camp at Barth, Germany on the northern peninsula.

Darbyshire suffered painful boils spread all over his body after sleeping outside on excelsior pads infected with ferocious sand fleas.

One incident Darbyshire described occurred when the POW guard in Barracks 7 was taking roll call. One of the prisoners answered a bit too slowly to the guard's liking. The guard started jabbing the POW with his bayonet, slipped and fell off the step, breaking his bayonet. Darbyshire chuckled recalling, "It was tough not to laugh hearing this German officer chew out the GI in English with this broken bayonet waving in the air."

When asked how he survived his nine-month ordeal, Darbyshire credited it with two things. "First, some of us POWs would have our own little church service among ourselves. We had no chaplain in our barracks so we would talk about the Bible—each one remembering different verses. That gave me a lot of strength."

Secondly, he claims to have been toughened by growing up on a farm in Southeastern Colorado during the "Dirty Thirties." Sometimes his family was reduced to eating horse meat and potatoes. Therefore, the POW diet of potatoes and dandelion leaves was not so different.

"Of course, we eyed a German officer who had a cat. We tried and tried to get that cat. One day we did. Guess where that cat ended up—in the dandelion stew!"

His POW group was liberated by Russians led by Marshall Zuchov. Afterwards, he recalled getting the drunkest he had ever been. Not in celebration, but in trying to keep peace with the Russians who had a reputation as hearty drinkers.

"I walked down a road trying to avoid meeting any Russians when a group of their officers pulled up a buckboard beside me. They passed me a jug; I drank out of it and handed it back. Then they proceeded to get out another one and passed it around.

"Later after getting away from them, I found a garage the Russians hadn't broken into yet, so I broke into it and 'borrowed' a big BMW motorcycle. When I came head-on to another vehicle, I took the ditch. I broke the cylinder off. How the handlebars missed me, I'll never know. I'd been dead if I wasn't so drunk."

Darbyshire made his way to camp Lucky Strike in France and waited for transport home. While there, he met General Eisenhauer, who visited the camp. Ike asked a GI for a mess kit. The GI didn't pay much attention to his request until Darbyshire flipped up Ike's collar displaying the General's stars.

Ike then sat at the table with Darbyshire and asked the group of GIs what they were "bitching about." When they replied they were anxious to get home, Ike assured them, "We'll get you boys home as soon as we can."

Shortly after that, they boarded a troop transport and shipped back to the US. Darbyshire was discharged as a First Sergeant in April of 1945 after serving in the US Army with the 192nd Bomb group in the 859 Bomb Squadron for 2 years 2 months and 16 days.

While in the service, Darbyshire was awarded several medals including: a weapons medal, POW medal, Air medal with 2 oak leaves, European theatre medal, 3 Battle stars, and a Good Conduct medal.

Returning to Lamar, Darbyshire worked at the Motor Supply machine shop. He joined the 947 Company of the National Guard, where he worked with several different pieces of artillery. He retired after 29 ½ years of service.

Darbyshire was active with the ex-POW organization, attending their state and national conferences. "Five of us who were held together as POW's in Stalag Luft 4 get together every year. In 1985 he attended the REFORGER in Europe where US, English, and French group got together for war games.

The first summer he served in the Guard some of the more inexperienced guys from a cross section of the military started harassing the group of veterans, including Darbyshire. A Captain Smith stepped in and warned them, "You want to play, go ahead, but this is a tough group of guys—all combat vets who returned alive!"

Let us give thanks for those who returned like First Sergeant Alfred Darbyshire.

Insight: "Even a cat-flavored dandelion stew can taste good."

Donald Wagner Survives German Prison Camp

That day, Sept. 12, 1944, went down in history as one during which a record number of American planes were shot down over German soil during World War II. Over fifty B17s went down. Donald Wagner from Holly, CO, was a flight engineer on one of those planes on their 13th Sortie mission, a 14-hour bombing run near Czechoslovakia. Wagner parachuted out, feeling thankful he landed in a plowed field, unlike their co-pilot who landed atop a rock fence.

Initially, Wagner was taken to a prison camp in Berlin and held in the basement. Then he was taken to Frankfurt for interrogation. At one point he was imprisoned in solitary confinement. The Germans thought he might be a spy because he had a "good German name like Wagner (Vagner)." On his birthday, Sept. 24, he was taken to Stalag Luft IV, northeast of Berlin, where he spent most of his imprisonment.

Wagner and the others suffered deplorable conditions in the prison camps. "Our breakfasts were one cup of hot water. For dinner, we got a half-cup of dehydrated kraut. The smell of that kraut was terrible. It reminded me of the time I was a kid and found an old dead horse lying in the pasture—that kraut smelled just like that rotting horse." The prisoners were also served potatoes intended for the pigs, with straw still stuck to the food. Most of the prisoners suffered from malnutrition.

In Feb. of '45 the prisoners were ordered to start The Black March. It was bitter cold. Wagner overheard one of the German officers give the order, "Take their damn shoes away and send them down the road." Wagner said his feet suffered severe frostbite, swelling larger than his boots.

He remembered staying in a barn along the way. "Being a farm boy, I knew if I could get up in the hayloft of that barn, I'd be warm. Sure enough, I got up there, buried myself in the hay. I slept all night long. It was the warmest bed I ever had in Germany."

Along the 90-day march, he contracted diphtheria and was taken to the hospital in New Brandenburg. Polish doctors cared for Wagner. One of his buddies was Polish and would interpret for him.

His outfit was liberated April 28. They stayed for another three weeks before an ambulance took them to a plane to fly to

Paris. Foul weather moved in, and they were delayed another four days.

After six weeks in Paris, Wagner was sent back to the US on a hospital ship, which docked in Newport News, West Virginia. From there, he was sent to Ft. Logan in Denver. He was discharged from the U.S. Air Corps on Sept. 26, 1945, two days after his birthday.

Two days later on Sept. 28, he married Dorothy, a young woman he met in KS., while he was working for Boeing. She was a teacher in Wichita. They met on a bus and dated before he was drafted on April 15, 1942.

After his induction, Wagner was sent to Dallas Aviation School, then onto New Orleans where he worked on B29s, getting them ready for training flights. He was later sent to Santa Anna, CA. to train as an Aviation Cadet and then to Radio School.

On July 4, 1943, his outfit, the 303 Bomb Group of the 360 Squadron, docked in England. Wagner was amused when a British gentleman informed him, "There is some sort of holiday going on in America today." (July 4th)

After Wagner was sent overseas, he continued his courtship with Dorothy through correspondence. She still has his letters, which he secretly confessed were "kind of mushy."

Before he shipped out, they devised a system to track his letters: on the first letter he used "Donald A. Wagner" in the return address. Each subsequent letter, he would change his middle initial to the next letter in the alphabet, "Donald B. Wagner, Donald C." etc. Using this system, she could tell if she was getting all his letters. "The letters quit coming after I received letter "L," Dorothy explained. "Then I knew he had either been killed or taken prisoner."

After their marriage, Mr. and Mrs. Wagner returned to Holly, CO, where he farmed until a few years ago when they moved to town. They have nine children: Donna, Barbara, David, twins Ronda and Rebecca, Thomas, Joseph, Steven, and Kevin. They are blessed with 20 grandchildren and one great grandchild.

One did not have to see the American flag resting in the corner of their living room to sense the pride Donald Wagner feels for America or the love of country he carried into battle and to that far away, cold, dark prison camp of World War II.

"If I hadn't been a strong-willed person, I'd never have made it," Wagner explained. "Yes, it was that and that guardian angel sitting on your shoulder," concluded Dorothy.

Insight: "It takes a strong-willed person to overcome adversity—and a guardian angel doesn't hurt either."

From the beet fields of Colorado to the beaches of Normandy, Elmer Sniff fights for freedom.

Around his hometown of Lamar, Colorado, Elmer Sniff is well known as a veterinarian. However, many of the locals do not realize Sniff is also one of the most highly decorated World War II veterans in Southeast Colorado. Among several other awards and honors, Sniff has been awarded the Bronze Star for heroism, the Purple Heart for being wounded in action, and the Silver Star for acts of gallantry. Sniff is most proud, however, of his Combat Infantry Badge. He earned this badge - a badge only given to those units, which actually fought in combat - while serving as a member of H Company of the 120th infantry regiment of the 30th infantry division.

His war efforts began as a student at Colorado State University in Fort Collins. Students were excused from classes to replace workers in the beet fields who had gone to war. After some of his friends were drafted, Sniff couldn't concentrate on his studies and decided to volunteer for induction into the Army in the spring of 1943.

He was sent to Camp Butner in North Carolina, for his Basic and Advanced training. Before going overseas, Sniff was also sent to the Tennessee Maneuvers Area and Camp Pickett, Virginia.

Sniff was working in Wales waterproofing vehicles, everything from jeeps to tanks, when the invasion of Normandy occurred. His unit sailed to Omaha Beach on the British HMS Donald Duck. (He delighted in the unusually whimsical name for a British vessel typically bearing much more dignified titles). They sailed throughout the night, landing on Omaha Beach on July 4, 1944.

As a machine gun specialist, Sniff carried the 48-pound gun while they attacked the beachhead.

"We dug in that night and kept our position for a week or more. Then they moved us back to a supposedly safer position. The planes came in right over us, and I was hit. This was on the 24th of July.

He was hospitalized near Hereford, England, a locale he found interesting because his parents raised Hereford cattle which originated from there.

In September, Sniff was sent back to his outfit in Holland, which was preparing to attack the fortified Siegfried Line along the German border.

"We broke through it and went into encircling action around the German city of Aachen. I stayed in a foxhole for six weeks, without a bath or shave. When we got out and hit the showers, we just stood there letting the hot water run over us. It took five or six shampoos to get all that red mud out of my hair."

They marched onward to the Ruhr River. They called off the attack, however, reasoning the Germans might blow up the dams they controlled along the river if they came under fire.

From there they were deployed to the Bulge. "It was at the Bulge, I saw my first buzz bombs. Sitting in a chalet, we would hear the whine of the bombs. Instinctively, we all reached for our helmets and put them on. I don't know what good our helmets would have done if we were actually hit."

After the Bulge, their unit was pulled back up and did cross the Ruhr.

"After that, the Germans seemed to lose some of their will to fight," Sniff recalled.

Sniff's unit continued, crossing the Rhine in storm boats.

Sniff finished his combat duty near Magdeburg along the Elbe River. It was here, on April 18, 1945, he earned the prestigious Silver Star. His commendation reads in part, "While advancing through an enemy town, Corporal Sniff's platoon was pinned down by automatic fire from a building. Corporal Sniff armed himself with a carbine and grenades and advanced alone by alternate rushing and creeping through heavy small arms fire to within twenty yards of the building. Exposing himself to point-blank fire, he hurled a grenade into the building. . . . Corporal Sniff's gallant act eliminated the enemy strongpoint, thereby enabling his platoon to advance."

His trip back home in August of 1945, only took five days, in the Queen Mary. The spacious ship was crowded with two regiments and three hospitals aboard. "We were double loaded. Two of us were assigned to one bunk, taking turns sleeping in the bunk one night and on deck the next."

One of the first things Sniff did upon arriving home was to marry Esther, his McClave high school sweetheart. "Sitting in that foxhole for six weeks, I couldn't get her out of my mind. I decided right then, I wanted to marry her," Sniff explains.

"Do you want to know the other half of the story?" Esther asks. Smiling sweetly, she takes Elmer's hand and continues, "At first I refused, but then God told me I'd made a big mistake, and I should marry Elmer. I'm so glad I did." That was over fifty-five years ago in March of 1946. They have been blessed with two sons, Clay and Neil, and a daughter, Leslie, three grandchildren and two great grandchildren.

Returning to CSU, Sniff graduated with a degree in Forestry and worked for the Bureau of Land Management for six and a half years, before deciding that was not for him. He and Esther then attended Washington State University. He earned his doctorate in Veterinarian Medicine and Esther a degree in Microbiology. Dr. Sniff operated a clinic in Lamar from March 1961 to Nov. 1988 and then did consulting work. "I still do some consulting work at places like the post office, but I just don't get paid for it," Sniff jokes.

The highly decorated Corporal Sniff courageously fought his way through places like Normandy, the Siegfried line, and the Bulge. In the hearts of people who know him, however, he will always be kind and gentle, Dr. Sniff.

Insight: "Prize more highly those medals earned as part of a team than those earned for individual acts of heroism."

Thomas Sandoval Fights with a "Win or Die" Attitude

Thomas Sandoval wasn't expected to live long enough to return to the United States after being wounded at Normandy, but his determined spirit and love for his wife carried him back home.

Sandoval worked at a hay mill before being inducted into the Army on Aug. 10, 1942. After basic training at Camp Walter, TX, he was assigned to the 35th Infantry Division as an ammunitions handler.

Back in Colorado, his sister died, and he was granted emergency leave to attend her funeral. It was a time of great sadness but also happiness. He seized the opportunity during that short window of time to marry his sweetheart, Carrie Hernandez of Las Animas, CO.

Then reality returned when the U.S. Army sent him to California then to New York as his point of exit to Europe and the beaches of Normandy.

He had been fighting across the hedgerows there for twenty-seven days on July 28, 1944, when the fighting intensified and things went from bad to worse.

"I didn't figure I was ever coming back when I saw my buddies lying all over. I thought, 'This is it, I'll either win or die.'" He stepped up to handle a thirty-five pound machine gun dropped by a fallen comrade.

On he fought, carrying the machine gun, two grenades, and his K rations. Suddenly he felt the breath sucked out of him as mortar shrapnel exploded through both sides of his chest. Fighting for survival on that wheat field, Sandoval struggled to get up. His buddy, Sandy, pushed him back down, "Don't move; don't get up; you'll just be a better target," Sandy ordered.

After lying there for what seemed like an eternity as he drifted in and out of consciousness, Sandoval was dragged 1500 yards to safety by another buddy, Woody.

At a field hospital, Sandoval began another long battle for his life. He had extensive chest and arm injuries and lost two ribs. He credits a can of K ration cheese with saving his life. "The shrapnel came at me from my right side but hit the can of cheese I carried, which slowed its progress. Otherwise it would have torn clear across to my heart, and that would've been it."

Infection set in due to a lack of penicillin. It looked like he might lose his battle. Reality blurred. "I remember lying there wishing I could just reach up and touch the clouds that hovered closer and closer overhead." But a force stronger than his wounds pulled him back.

When he had recovered sufficiently to make the trip, they loaded him on a gurney and shipped him back to the United States. He spent eighteen months at the Bushnell General Army Hospital in Brigham City, Utah. His wife, Carrie, quickly came to his side, encouraging him through the long road to recovery.

Sandoval was discharged on Nov. 8, 1945. He returned to Lamar, where he worked for fourteen years at the WHO Milling Company as a dehydrator operator. He also worked for eighteen years at Western Alfalfa in Granada, CO.

It wasn't until he was fifty-seven years old, that a representative from the Disabled American Veterans helped him get disability retirement.

Sandoval's life revolves around his family. Remarkably, he and Carrie have nineteen children: Thomas Anthony, Victor, Antonia, Ted, Rebecca, Pamela, Felix, Larry, Janie, Sandy, Tomasita, Barbara, Frankie, Francis, Alex, Andrew, Maggie, Raymond, and Caroline. Counting successive generations becomes complicated in a hurry, but Sandoval has sixty grandkids and "70 or so" great grandkids. Family reunions not only fill the house, but their yard and neighborhood as well.

Surrounded by his family and large assortment of pets, Thomas Sandoval reflected over his full life. The hedgerows of Normandy recede into a long and distant past. He definitely won the battle—and won it with honor and distinction.

Insight: "Even a piece of cheese can be a lifesaver, if it's in the right place at the right time."

Saldana Family Suffers A Double Tragedy

World War II dealt a double tragedy to the family of Refugio and Bessie Saldana, who raised twelve children, 8 sons and 4 daughters, in Prowers County, CO. Lawrence, the second oldest, was killed during the Battle of Normandy, and Nick, the fourth oldest, was permanently disabled.

Lawrence was working for John Dashner when he was inducted into the Army in 1943. He completed basic training and returned home on furlough, seeing his family for the last time. He then rejoined the U.S. 1st Army under General Omar Bradley, which was part of the Allied forces crossing the English Channel on D-Day, June 6, 1944 to establish beachheads at Normandy, France. Lawrence was one of 176,00 Allied soldiers from Britain, Canada, and U.S. who stormed the beaches that day to thwart the progress of Hitler as he marched on the European continent. Lawrence was a sharpshooter in the infantry, qualified in both rifle and submachine gun operation.

    The U.S. troops Lawrence fought with met with strong German resistance on Omaha beach. Fierce fighting continued as the Allied forces pressed inland during June and July. Although the mission was hailed by some as the turning point in the war, many heroic soldiers lost their lives.

    Lawrence's family received word that "The burial of Private First Class Lawrence T. Saldana was at the U.S. Military Cemetery, Blosville, France, plot K, row 8, grave 144. The cemetery is located approximately 20 miles northwest of St. Lo, 24 miles southeast of Cherboug and 5 miles north and slightly west of Carentan, all in France. With sincere sympathy, Major General T.

B. Larkin." Lawrence Saldana was 19 years old when he was killed.

For his heroic and meritorious achievement, Lawrence was awarded the Bronze Star as well as the Purple Heart, for wounds received in action resulting in his death, July 3, 1944.

Nick Saldana, Lawrence's younger brother, entered the Army and completed his basic training at Ft. Bliss, Texas. Shortly thereafter, he was disabled and returned to Colorado. He received care at Fitzsimmons Veteran's Hospital in Denver and, later, at Ft. Lyon. Currently, he is under the care of his sister, Rebecca Alba, in Lamar.

During a ceremony commemorating the 50th Anniversary of D-Day, both brothers were awarded the Jubilee of Liberty medal.

The medal represents Normandy. On the front "Overlord 6 June 1944" is inscribed on the upper part of the medal, with the flag of the Allied Countries and the names of the landing beaches completing the face of the medal. On the reverse side of the medal is the Torch of Freedom surrounded by the device of William the Conqueror "Diex aie" (God is with us).

After World War II, three other Saldana brothers, Andrew, John, and Joe also served in the military.

The Saldana family proudly and heroically served the United States of America during World War II and following. Their lives and faces reflect the often-repeated phrase describing WW II veterans, "All gave, some gave all.

Insight: "All gave some, some gave all."

LeRoy Nickelson Leads the Charge

Saint Lo was still smoldering when the 557th Field Artillery battalion arrived at Normandy about a month after D-Day. First Lieutenant LeRoy Nickelson Jr., Executive Officer of Battery C (Charley), led his 110 men in helping to roust out the Germans.

First the military sent in aircraft. For a week the skies were darkened with wave after wave of planes flying in, strafing the French village of Brest, south of Normandy. The town was utterly destroyed. The German soldiers, however, were holed up underground and still presented a formidable threat.

"So we decided to take them the old-fashioned way, by sending in the artillery," explained Nickelson. "That was us, the suicide troop, as we were called.

"The United States military put obsolete guns on obsolete tanks and made them the finest war machines in the world," explained Nickelson. "These guns would fire a 5 inch shell 9 miles and sink a cruiser at the range of 5 miles. It could be ready to fire in two minutes and accomplish our mission in five."

Nickelson's Battery led the charge in two direct fire missions at Brest. Their mission was to destroy the observation tower. The strong point of the tower was situated just below the crest of a hill. Direct fire from a distance hit too high on the tower to do any damage. Nickelson made the decision to bring their artillery, with a 19-foot barrel, up to within 100 yards of the tower. "We fired five rounds and completely destroyed it."

The second mission was on the beach. The Germans had turned their coastal defense guns away from the sea and were firing on American troops. "Their guns were much bigger than ours," recalled Nickelson.

Refuting orders from two infantry officers, Nickelson mapped a different strategy. "The infantry wanted me to take my guys in following a route where we would be under direct German observation for about a mile and stay there until we suffered about a third casualties. I reconnoitered another attack. We hit them from a parallel front, where they couldn't see us coming. We hit them hard and got out fast. The infantry also got out fast, so fast they dropped some candy bars. We didn't get out so fast that we didn't stop and pick up that candy!"

After evacuating all his sweet-toothed men first, Nickelson made his escape by clinging to a retreating jeep's spare tire.

That night Nickelson's Battery returned and fired at the Germans from behind a hill. "We fired all night, until the paint peeled off our guns." One confused American soldier somehow found himself forward of the firing line. He dug himself into a hole and survived. "After that, he stayed so close to me, he was a nuisance," Nickelson quipped.

When the smoke cleared, over 80,000 Germans surrendered to our relentless American onslaught, surpassing the American military intelligence estimate of 28,000.

Nickelson recounted several other near misses on his life. "Guess I was just lucky," he reasoned. "Lucky and steely on the inside."

He described one incident near the Belgium/German border. His battery had merged with a column of American tanks when German gunfire suddenly exploded around them. "I still remember that terrifying sound of those bullets ricocheting off those tanks," he recalled.

Battery C took cover in a house with 200 or 300 other GI's. German artillery hit one of the tanks, blowing the tank commander out of the turret. Nickelson could hear his plaintive cries as he clung precariously to the side of the tank, "Come get me, Daddy."

Nickelson called for a volunteer, and they raced out under fire and rescued the soldier off the tank. All three survived.

Nickelson described how he faced going into combat. "I wasn't afraid of dying. I forced myself to think about our mission and how we were going to accomplish it. I worried, instead, about the small stuff, like making silly mistakes.

"Our outfit had such a good record in Europe, they were going to send us to Tokyo Bay. We were back in the States waiting to be shipped to Japan when the atomic bombs were dropped, ending the war. We weren't sorry to see it end."

LeRoy Nickelson returned a hero to Prowers County in 1946.

He received the highest efficiency rating in his battalion. "They offered to send me to staff school to become a major. Instead, I came home."

Nickelson had a wife, Wyona, and a daughter, Anita May, waiting at home. Anita was born one month after he was drafted in 1942. After the war, he and Wyona had three more daughters and a son.

Nickelson had graduated from the University of Colorado in 1940 with a degree in Geology and worked in the Louisiana oil fields before the war. He returned to help his father farm. He used his geology education for a short time teaching historical geology at Lamar Community College and advised the city of Lamar how to provide safe drinking water after the '65 flood.

Today, Nickelson enjoys growing fruit on his place west of Lamar, which is teeming with fruit and nut trees, grapevines, and strawberry plants. When asked how he keeps the birds away, Nickelson shook his head, "I don't. Mostly Orioles come around, and I just don't have it in me to shoot them."

Although a gentle, congenial gardener, First Lieutenant C. LeRoy Nickelson is indeed, "steely on the inside" courageously earning his Bronze Star for "distinguished, heroic meritorious service against the enemy in France and Germany."

Insight: "I wasn't afraid of dying. I worried, instead, about the small stuff—like making silly mistakes."

Laurencio Via Comes Home A Hero

During his military career in World War II, Laurencio Via of Lamar served as a rifleman with the 7th A.I. Battalion in the 3rd Army. He used rifle, grenade, and bayonet in guard and company duty in combat throughout Germany, France, and Luxemborg, earning the Bronze Star and the Purple Heart.

Via was born in New Mexico. When he was a month old, his mother died, and he was sent to live with his grandmother. At eighteen years of age, he was drafted into military service on Oct. 13, 1943.

He was sent first to Fort Bliss in Texas then on to Fort Roberts in California, for Basic Training. When the rest of his group was shipped out, the military lost Via's papers so he had to remain behind.

"But it worked out good. All the others had to go to Japan. I didn't want to go to Japan." Via remembers. "So when they lost my papers, I missed being sent there and was granted a short furlough in New Mexico instead."

After the military relocated his papers, they sent Via to Germany with Company B of the 320th Infantry.

During one of his first days in Germany, his company was marching at night. Suddenly enemy sniper fire erupted in the dark. Laurencio was hit in the right arm near his shoulder. His sergeant was also hit. They laid low all during that night. The next morning the General arrived.

"The General was talking, and I was listening," explained Via, "when all of a sudden, that sniper shot one of the stars off the General's shoulder. He wasn't hurt but didn't return fire because he didn't want the sniper to know his exact location."

While Via recovered in the evac hospital, he was awarded the Purple Heart, the oldest military decoration in the world in present use. The Purple Heart was designed by order of George Washington to be awarded to combat wounded veterans.

Although the experience frightened Via, he didn't hesitate to go back into combat.

During one effort to roust the Germans from their positions, Via described getting within twenty feet of the enemy. "We were walking through the grass yelling. Suddenly this German stood up, threw down his bazooka, and surrendered. The German said he'd rather take his chances with us than fire that thing, because it knocked down whoever was holding it as well as its target. "

The incident that earned Via his Bronze Star, a military decoration for heroic actions, occurred after his company had captured several German soldiers who were hiding in a house. While the sergeant guarded them, Via reentered the house, single-handedly capturing a German soldier who had escaped discovery earlier.

While Via's outfit transported the Germans to a POW camp, he stayed with one of them who was crippled. "I found him a stick to use," Via said, "so he could walk faster and keep up with the rest of them."

Via described his war experience, "Some days were a lot of fun; others were not as good as they looked."

The last day he was in Germany, Via earned his promotion to sergeant. Since he was such a short timer, Via unselfishly relinquished his promotion to a close friend, rather than keeping it for himself.

He returned to the U.S. on the Queen Mary. "It was a smooth three-day journey compared to seventeen days of rough seas on the ship we went over on." Via described.

On that last journey, another incident occurred that underscored the trauma of war. One of the soldiers in his company became despondent when talking about the war and jumped overboard. Efforts were made to rescue him, but his body was never found.

Via was discharged Nov. 11, 1945 from Camp Breckenridge, Kentucky.

Whether fighting for his country overseas or helping children here at home, Laurencio Via is a hero in the truest sense of the word.

Insight: "Some days were a lot of fun; others weren't as good as they looked. You were there for one purpose—either hit of get hit."

Jewell Seufers Answers the Cry for Help in the Pacific

September 3, 1942-Jewell Seufer should have been starting his senior year in high school. Instead, he and a friend, Eddy Leonard, went to Denver and enlisted in the Navy. The next morning they were on a train to San Diego, but were separated after their two weeks of basic training.

Jewell was assigned to the 2nd Marines as a Navy Corpsman and sent to the Central Pacific where he landed on five beachheads and cared for soldiers on the front lines in some of the bloodiest battles of the war.

At 2:15 A.M. on November 20, 1943, the soldiers were given last rites aboard ship. Shortly thereafter, Seufer and the Marines hit Betio beach on the Tarawa Atoll. "We landed at low tide, 500 yards out," Seufer later described to a family member. "We tried to wade ashore over sharp coral reefs. We couldn't get in the trees, and the Japs were gunning us down." Few of the first wave survived.

The fighting continued for the next three days. "Jewell had to crawl on his belly up to the front lines and administer first aid to the wounded," his Aunt Ena related his account of the battle. "He was totally shocked and saddened when he found his buddy slumped up against a tree. All he could do to help the wounded was give them morphine."

The Marines eventually took the island, but not without a bloody price. In the 76-hour fight for Betio, 1056 Marines and sailors were killed or were missing. Some 2300 were wounded but recovered. Only 17 of Seufer's platoon survived.

Seufer was wounded with shrapnel and later awarded the Purple Heart. However, he never received his medal as the Navy sent it to a port after he had shipped out for another assignment. It never caught up with him. Seufer was too humble to pursue tracking it down.

Suefer's next battle was at Saipan, where the headquarters for the Japanese Pacific Fleet was located. The battle raged from June 15, 1944 to July 9 before the Americans took the island.

From there, Seufer was sent to Tinian to assist the 2nd Marines in that invasion. Enemy opposition was not strong, and by the time the Japanese gathered in force to counterattack, the Marines were firmly established. Tinian offered the best site in the Marianas for the extra-long runways required by the B-29s. From the Atoll of Tinian Island, a single B-29 bomber took off in August of 1945 with a single bomb aboard that would spell the end of World War II.

Seufer served in two other Pacific battles as a Navy Corpsman with the 2nd Marines, the battle to retake Guam and the Battle of the Philippine Sea.

The cry, "Corpsman," rang out in every naval operation in the Pacific. When these words were uttered by a wounded or dying Marine, it was an immediate call to action for Jewell Seufer.

"Jewell never wanted to talk about his war experiences," his wife, Dorothy, explained. "He would relate funny stories that happened but was reluctant to speak of the fighting."

During his service in the Pacific, Seufer could not contact his family back in Holly, CO. His mother, Lelia frantic with worry sat on the edge of her bed, sobbing and pounding her knees at night. Hearing that Eleanor Roosevelt made a visit to the troop hospitals in the Pacific, Lelia wrote her asking if she had seen Jewell. Surprisingly, Eleanor Roosevelt wrote her back, responding that she had met many of the corpsmen, but did not know their names.

Seufer was stationed at the Naval Hospital at Sun Valley, Idaho, for the last year of his service. While there, he returned to Holly, Colorado, to marry Dorothy Leonard, a sister of his buddy who enlisted at the same time he did.

Dorothy related a few dietary quirks of Jewell's resulting from his wartime experience. He couldn't eat chocolate or pineapple juice. Apparently during one of the battles, he had existed for four days eating only a chocolate bar. Later, he "overdosed" on a crate of pineapple juice some buddies "lifted" from a ship.

After his discharge, Oct.18, 1945, Jewell spent the rest of his life farming and ranching near Holly. Dorothy and Jewell have five children: Donald and Dale farm near Holly, Delaine (Dunning) works as a school nurse for the county, Greg manages the Coolidge Dairy, and JoLynne works for the Agricultural Department in Spokane, Washington.

The contribution Jewell Seufer made to the war effort lives on in the hearts of his family and the myriad of country friends who knew and loved him. Somewhere, walking the country lanes and city streets of America, are countless numbers of ex-Marines who owe their lives to Jewell Seufer, the Navy Corpsman who bandaged their wounds during the heat of battle.

Insight: "Do the best you can at everything and you will be O.K. (from a letter he wrote home from the war to his mother)

Darrell Seufer Follows His Brother to the Pacific

Cinders poured from the smoke stack of the coal-powered train as it made its way across the U.S. The G.I's aboard all kept their windows open for a breath of cool air, even though the invading soot blackened their skin. As the train passed through Holly, CO., Darrell Seufer spotted his father-in-law about a block from the tracks and called out a greeting. He was quickly  reprimanded for giving away his unit's location and made to shut his window for the next 80 miles.

Earlier in Dec.1944, Darrell Seufer had interrupted his farming and ranching career north of Holly to enlist in the Navy. His older brother, Jewell, had just returned from the war in the Pacific.

Seufer's ship was half way across the Pacific en route to Japan, when word reached them the U.S. had bombed Nagasaki and Hiroshima. Turning back, his ship headed for the Philippines.

On the Philippines, Seufer spotted his brother-in-law, Jack Nazarenus in the chow line. They requested to be sent together for their next assignment. The Navy sent Nazarenus home and Seufer to Truk Island.

With no dock in the harbor, Seufer's ship, the first American ship on Truk Island, beached 1000 feet from dry land. The military directed the 45,000 surrendered Japanese soldiers on the island to hand-carry rocks to construct a landing ramp for the heavy equipment on board.

During the two or three weeks this took to complete, Seufer slept on the ship's deck. Even for a seasoned cowboy like Seufer, solid steel did not make a very comfortable bedroll. He was thankful to move to a tent for the remaining nine months.

One night when the sailors all slept soundly, several Japanese snuck into their tent and stole much of their gear. Consequently, the GI's piled all their belongings onto their cot with them.

Seufer belonged to the Seabees whose job was to widen the one-mile-wide island enough to allow large transports and bombers to land. Day after day, Seufer labored packing down ground rock and dirt, enlarging the island ¼ to ½ mile in width. Ironically, no planes ever landed on the specially constructed airstrip.

One day while exploring some of caves on the island, Seufer spotted a Japanese sword. Somehow that sword made its way home with Seufer.

Although eligible to be shipped home earlier, Seufer had to wait several months for a ship to come get him. Even then, their departure was ill timed. The thirteen small LCI ships, the smallest ocean-going vessels in the Navy, hit heavy rain a half day out from port. Soon a typhoon engulfed their ship. "The waves looked just like the Rocky Mountains," Seufer described. "For three days and nights, we stayed below deck with the hatch shut. We could hear the prop come out of the water and plunge back downward. I vowed if I ever got back to Prowers County, I'd never get in a boat again, and I never have. That water will flat out kill you."

Fortunately, Seufer survived, although one of the ships in their convoy succumbed to the fury of the storm. At the Philippines, Seufer transferred to a larger ship for the trip back to the States. Seufer later described the Philippines as "very beautiful; they'd make great cow pastures."

Seufer returned to Holly and his farming, ranching operation. For sixteen years, he served Prowers County as County Commissioner.

He is also well known for his excellent horses. One of his paint running mares, Misty Moon, was a champion, winning 19 out of 22 races.

Seufer remarried. He and his wife, Mary Lou, had two daughters and one son. One of their daughters, Becky, married a wheat farmer and lives near Syracuse, KS. She rodeos and was named Kansas State Champion Break Away Roper by the Professional Rodeo Assoc. in 1999. Their other daughter, Peggy (Kalma) lives north of Holly and is an accomplished artist.

Their son, Tommy, is a pharmacist in Canon City. He also has a nursery. One day, he overstocked on trees and brought the surplus to his dad in Holly. Thus, Darrell got started in the tree business.

"I've lived about four lives since riding that train on my way to becoming a Navy Seabee: farmer/rancher, cowboy, tree farmer, and county commissioner," quipped Seufer. "Guess that just goes to show, I can do about anything I make up my mind to do."

Insight: "I can do anything I make up my mind to do."

Howard Ragsdale Fights in the Okinawa Foxholes

As a young married farmer from Halfway, Mo., Howard Ragsdale received his draft notice to report to the U.S. Army on September 28, 1942, to assist his country's troops in World War II. He left his pregnant wife, Mary Jane, with corn in the field and hogs in the pen. She had to rely on neighbors and relatives for assistance in harvesting and feeding. An auction of his farm equipment was held prior to his leaving.

Howard reported to Camp Adair, Oregon, and went through training in several camps in Oregon, Washington, and California. His 96th Division nicknamed "The Deadeyes," was an artillery group, employing 25mm canons. Howard related to family members how quickly they could tear down their equipment, relocate and set it up again, "I could do it in my sleep."

The 96th loaded ship in San Francisco, CA., and shipped out with amphibious landing craft to the front lines on Leyte Island in the Philippines. However, as the troops were landing, Howard had an attack of appendicitis, had emergency surgery, and had to stay on board ship.

Howard said he was the "oldest and shortest private." He was almost thirty and recalled having trouble keeping the marching pace "with those Texans, whose legs extended to their Adams Apples."

Howard was involved with the Okinawa campaign and vividly recalled sitting in dark foxholes listening to the incessant shellfire, grenade explosions, and screams in the endless nights, not knowing where the next explosion would be or who might jump into his foxhole. The Japanese would arm themselves with grenades and jump into a foxhole with American GI's, or they would quickly jump in and out of the foxhole hoping to confuse the American soldiers into firing at their own. His infantry unit numbered 2800 and acquired 2480 casualties.

Howard recalled seeing Gen. Douglas McArthur passing in a jeep while his unit was guarding a bridge.

He was honorably discharged on Dec. 21, 1945, at Fort Leavenworth, KS., and returned to his family in Halfway, MO. As typical for World War II soldiers, who were separated from family, Howard had seen his oldest son very little and had never seen his one and a half year old. Shortly after his discharge, he was diagnosed with malaria -a souvenir from the Philippines.

In 1946, the Ragsdale family traveled to southeastern Colorado and settled first near Granada and then later moved to Lamar, where he was engaged in dryland wheat farming and raising cattle south of town.

Howard and Mary raised seven children and were active members of the Lamar community.

Howard was proud of his participation in the military service and the good that it accomplished, but he was certainly glad to have completed his tour of duty and return to farming. He often told family and friends that he hoped the United States would live in peace, and he certainly did not want to go through another war.

Insight: "We could all make this world a better place if we each lived in peace with our neighbor."

Harold V. Smith Courageously Saves Lives

When Harold V. Smith joined the National Guard in 1940, he had no delusions of becoming a hero. He was just hoping to make a few extra dollars to help out with expenses.

However, in a few short months Smith was thrust into the bloodiest battle in history as the United States became involved in World War II in 1941. Suddenly, he was a clerk in the medical detachment of the 157th Infantry, 45th Division.

Since his early childhood, Smith had been taking care of people, such as his elderly grandparents, who ran the mill in Lamar.

Nov. 7, 1944, Smith was awarded the Silver Star for acts of gallantry. His commendation read: "Lieutenant Smith was in charge of the battalion aid station when the area was hit by enemy artillery fire. Despite the exploding shells which killed the battalion surgeon, wounded several men, and knocked Lieutenant Smith to the ground, he immediately assumed the duties of assistant battalion surgeon and began to administer blood plasma and give first aid treatment. He did not seek cover until all the wounded had been cared for and evacuated. Lieutenant Smith's gallant conduct assisted in saving the lives of several wounded men and reflects credit on the Army of the United States."

While serving in battles in Africa, Sicily, Italy, Germany, and France, Smith earned several additional medals including the Purple Heart, when he was wounded with shrapnel in the left chest near Pozzilli, Italy, Nov. 24, 1943.

His service to country and community did not end when he was discharged Aug. 30, 1945. Smith returned to Lamar and worked in the flourmill for a time. He continued to serve as Commanding Officer of the National Guard unit in Lamar and then spent several years in the Reserve unit in LaJunta, CO., retiring with the rank of Major.

Moving to Wiley, CO., Smith worked in the State Bank of Wiley, a job he held for approximately forty years. He was described as a much-loved man who understood people that didn't have great sums of money and treated everyone fairly.

He served on the City Council for several years and later, as Mayor of Wiley.

His wife, Betty, taught school in Wiley. They had one daughter, Marge Lubbers, who also teaches school in Wiley.

Although he didn't set out to be one, Harold V. Smith, returned and remained, a hometown hero.

Insight: "Care for the wounded around you before seeking shelter for yourself."

Fern Morgan R.N. Does the Right Thing

Thinking it was the right thing to do, Fern Morgan RN enlisted in the Army Air Corps in July, 1942. She wanted to do what she could to help the war effort.

Born in Cleveland, OH, Morgan graduated from the West Suburban Hospital School of Nursing in Oak Park, IL.

While serving with the Army Air Corps, Morgan worked at the Selfridge Field 25th Evacuation Hospital in Selfridge, Michigan. Morgan served in all areas of the hospital during her tour of duty. She became accustomed to taking the initiative, making quick decisions, and adopting innovative solutions to a broad range of medical-related problems.

Morgan was one of 59,000 American nurses who served in the Army Nurse Corps, as it was later named, during World War II. World War II was the largest and most violent armed conflict in the history of mankind. Within the "chain of evacuation" established by the Army Medical Department during the war, nurses served under fire in field hospitals and evacuation hospitals, on hospital trains and hospital ships, and as flight nurses on medical transport planes. The skill and dedication of Morgan and the other nurses contributed to the extremely low post-injury mortality rate among American military forces in every theater of the war, as well as in the States. Overall, fewer than 4 percent of the American soldiers who received medical care in the field or underwent evacuation died from wounds or disease.

In October 1943, Morgan married Dr. Edward Fenimore, a major in the Army. At that time, women who married were discharged from military service.

Morgan continued her nursing career, working in the field of pediatrics in N.J. and Ky. In 1966, she was invited to speak at the National Conference of the Amercian College of Obstetrics and Gynecology.

Morgan raised one son, David, who lives in Phoenix, AZ and two daughters, Debby, who resides in Birmingham, AL., and

Candy Ruedeman from Lamar. Morgan inspired her daughter Candy to become a RN, a dream born in Candy when she was 5 years old.

Morgan was always proud that she could contribute something of service to her country as an Army nurse.

Insight: "We can all help our country in some way."

Judge Sanderson
Endures Misjudgement by the U.S. Army

Robert Sanderson, Judge Sanderson—as most folks in southeastern Colorado know him—entered this life during the heat of summer, 1918, in the small town of Higbee, Missouri.

A brother joined the family two years later. Tragically, his mother died of peritonitis a short time later when Robert was only two and half years old. Since his father was a lineman for Southwestern Bell Telephone Company, and his work demanded a move to a different town every few weeks, he and his brother were raised by his maternal grandparents. He describes his young childhood as "delightful- we could not have had better caretakers." Sanderson lived with his grandparents during the school year, often traveling with his father during the summer.

When he was nineteen, Sanderson got a job in Kansas City, MO., at Jones Store as a stock boy in the rug department. It was his job to deliver rugs from the fourth floor to the third floor when needed. Since there were no operators in the elevators, the stock boys kept a heavy piece of wire handy to reach inside the elevator and open the door. One day when he needed to take some rugs down, he ran up and down the stairs until he found the elevator. Taking it to the fourth floor, he hid the wire, hurriedly retrieved his cart with rugs, and returned to the elevator. Assuming the elevator was still there because he had hid the wire, he opened the door, walked in and fell three floors to the basement. Someone, somehow, had moved the elevator.

He was taken to a nearby hospital where he lay unconscious for three days, not expected to live. His injuries were extensive: a fractured right ankle, fractured vertebrae, fractured skull, facial injuries, and a concussion. Eventually he did recover, but sustained irreparable damage to his optic nerve, resulting in 20/100 vision in his left eye and 20/200 vision in his right eye, qualifying him as legally blind in that eye.

When he turned twenty-one, the department store let him go. He moved to Chicago, where his brother had a job for him with the railroad.

He was drafted in 1942. When he took his physical, Sanderson could not read the eye chart. Believing he was malingering, the Army accepted him and sent him to B24 maintenance school in Oklahoma City because he did so well on his aptitude tests.

"I couldn't tell a tailpipe from a carburetor," Sanderson confessed. "But they thought I was doing so well, they promoted me to a P38 Specialist."

Ordering him to pack up his winter uniforms, the Army sent him to New York City in the dead of winter. Continuing, he shipped out to the South Pacific, going through the Panama Canal to Caledonia, where it was hot, humid, and summertime.

From there, he went to Espiritu Santo in the New Hebrides Isles. He survived an earthquake there, only to come down with dengue fever. When the rest of his unit of the 321 Service Group with the 13th Air Force went north to the fighting, Sanderson was sent to the naval hospital to recover. "I got to eat the Navy's fresh food, while the other guys in my outfit were eating SPAM," Sanderson quipped.

After his recovery, Sanderson was sent to the Admiralty Islands and then to Zimboanga on Mindanao in the southern Philippines to rejoin the 13th Air Force. From there, they advanced north toward Japan.

"The Army would go in first and establish a beach head or land force. Then the engineers and the Seebees would go in and set up an airstrip," Sanderson explained. "We were next to move in to fix the airplanes. We'd camp on the edge of the airstrip in bunkers set up every 400 yards."

Sanderson recalls an experience his 9th Service Squadron had on Morotai Island in the Halmahera Archipelago in the Dutch

East Indies. "We were on a small transport ship with much of our equipment stored on the lower level of the hold. I was assigned to help unload them. While down in the hold, I heard gunfire and what I thought were bombs. I rushed up to the deck in time to see one of the Japanese planes attacking us from the west or starboard side. I didn't want to be killed, so I ran around the cabins and the bridge where I'd be somewhat protected from gunfire. When I got portside, I could see the beach and the Japanese bombers flying in to drop their deadly cargo. I thought since we were one of the first ships in, we would surely go down.

"Suddenly intense gunfire erupted from the batteries set up by our forces. I saw at least one of the Japanese planes go down. Apparently the Navy and Advance Forces had prepared defensive forces for our arrival. I must say they did an excellent job."

Another memorable incident occurred also while he was on Morotai. His brother, George, was a crew chief for a fighter squadron with the 8th Air Force stationed in New Guinea. He knew where Robert was and convinced a B25 pilot who was flying north of Morotai to take him over to see Robert. "He arrived without notice and surprised me. The other guys in my tent set up a cot for him. We got to be together for a couple days before the pilot returned to take him back to New Guinea. That meant so much because we were very close. Even though he was younger, I relied on him very much." George also returned from the war, but was later killed in the States.

Sanderson was discharged in October 1945.

Seeking an education, Sanderson enrolled in a Methodist university in Oklahoma City. There he met and married his wife, Vida. He then transferred to Oklahoma University in Norman, OK. After graduation, he moved to Colorado to get out of the OK heat and humidity and attended law school at the University of Colorado.

There was an opening in District Attorney Wilke Ham's office in Springfield, CO. Sanderson worked there for fourteen years before becoming District Judge in Lamar, CO., in 1966. Before his retirement in 1984, he was very active in the American Bar Association, traveling to many of their conventions.

Sanderson recalled spending much of his military time pulling K.P. duty because the Army thought he wasn't doing his job right. In reality, he was functioning far above the level his damaged eyesight afforded.

    The U.S. Army may have unfairly judged Robert Sanderson on several different occasions. He did not dwell on the "what ifs" of his life, however; instead he put all his energy into becoming the best he could be- in the military and as an honorable attorney and Judge in Southeast Colorado.

Insight: "Even the fairest of judges may be unfairly judged by others."

Jack Hall Chooses to Care

Jack Hall, a Lamar native, was working as a brand inspector in the Trinidad area when he received a letter from Uncle Sam "congratulating" him because "your friends and neighbors have selected you to represent them in the conflict" (World War II), as Hall states it. On May 19, 1942, Hall was inducted in the U.S. Army and traveled to Camp Barkley near Abilene, TX, for basic training.

From there, he was assigned to the 7th Surgical Hospital (SH) at Fort Ord near Monterey, CA. Hall served as a surgical technician, first on the wards and later in the operating rooms preparing instruments and packs for surgery.

The 7th SH was a 400-bed hospital, set up to operate out of semi-trailers. However, due to difficulty maneuvering those big rigs in tight quarters in the field, the semis were soon abandoned, and the unit was renamed the 92nd Evacuation Hospital S.M. (semi-mobile).

Their first assignment was in the Mojave Desert to care for General Patton's 3rd and 5th Armored Divisions. The General himself was treated for heat stroke. When asked what it was like to have Patton for a patient, Hall explained, "All officers left their rank at the door of the hospital."

The 92nd SM was shipped to Australia, serving both at Brisbane and Rockhampton. Their first invasion was at Hollandia, New Guinea. They suffered very few casualties; however, the Japanese did drop "a lucky bomb" on their food and supplies.

Their second invasion, at Biak, New Guinea started off uneventful as they established a beachhead. When they tried to reach an airstrip about a mile away, however, they discovered the Japanese were in caves all along the route, shelling the road. Within

1½ hours of landing at Biak, the 92nd SM was operational and had a patient on the operating table.

The 92nd relocated to a small island across the lagoon, Owi. Although unknown at the time, the island was infested with a mite that carried the disease Scrub Typhus. In one day, they admitted over 1100 sick soldiers.

The 92nd SM was part of a convoy of ships that took part in the invasion of Luzon, a northern island in the Philippines. Traveling past the perimeter of the US Defense Zone, they entered "no-man's land" and set up their hospital at Guimba in a school. They had no protection from supporting troops and were forced to man their own defense perimeter.

The afternoon of Jan. 31, 1945 the 6th Rangers brought in 911 U.S. soldiers who were prisoners of war from Camp Cabanatuan and who had survived the Death March of 1942. Many of the soldiers were weak with Beri-beri, a nerve disease caused by a defiency of vitamin B. All the prisoners were emaciated, and several had complicated medical conditions. The American POW Commanding Officer was Colonel Stillwell, a brother of "Vinegar Joe Stillwell," of Burma fame. General MacArthur came to welcome the prisoners.

President Truman had authorized the use of the atomic bomb, which destroyed the cities of Hiroshima and Nagasaki, Japan on Aug. 6 and 9, 1945.

On Sept. 2, 1945, the 92nd SM troops heard the ceremony of surrender aboard the USS Missouri in Tokyo Bay.

Hall then helped pack and ready the 92nd SM to follow the 25th Division to Nagoyo, Japan to care for the casualties. They were in Wakayama Bay during a typhoon. After being aboard ship for over 30 days, they traveled to Nagoyo to unload. Hall and approximately 28 other soldiers had enough points to be sent home without serving in the hospital in Japan.

Hall arrived on Angel Island, in San Francisco Bay in time for Thanksgiving 1945. "The Golden Gate Bridge was the last thing we saw leaving the US and the first thing we saw coming home," remembers Hall. He was discharged Nov. 28, 1945.

After the war, Hall married Bonnie and had three daughters, Betty, Mary, and Jamie. Among other jobs, he served as county assessor for 28 years from Jan. 13, 1959 to Jan. 13, 1987.

Hall volunteered time for the "Meals on Wheels" program and, served as Treasurer of the Prowers Co. Historical Society. He spent a large portion of his time working on his family's genealogy.

Jack Hall did, indeed, represent his Lamar friends and neighbors, as well as the whole United States, during World War II, and he did so with courage, dignity, and honor.

Insight: "Even the highest decorated officer, left his rank at the door of the hospital."

Ray Estrada Serves As A Role Model for Future Generations

Service to country is an Estrada family tradition. Three Estrada brothers fought simultaneously in the Pacific arena during World War II. Bart, a Navy man, served on a minesweeper. Nick served with the 8th Cavalry and Ray with the Americal Division of the 8th Army. A fourth brother was inducted, but not called up due to a physical problem. Most importantly, all three Estrada brothers returned home safely.

Ray Estrada lives in Granada, CO, now and has for several decades. When World War II broke out, he lived with his parents and thirteen siblings in California. After he was drafted in April 1943, he completed Basic Training in Alabama. He returned briefly to CA. before being shipped to the Pacific.

His first tour of duty was on Bougainville Island in Papua, New Guinea, where his Americal Infantry Division "mopped up the island, going after a few stragglers" as Ray described.

He remembers when McArthur landed on the Philippines with those now famous words, "I have returned." Ray was already there, having been shipped to the Philippines a short time earlier. "McArthur was my general," Estrada recalls, "I had a lot of respect for that man."

October 14, 1944 Estrada's Americal unit invaded Leyte. Estrada filled a highly dangerous position, hauling ammunition to the front lines. "There were snipers everywhere. They'd hide in the coconut trees," Estrada remembers. "Once our air support came in and strafed a bunch of coconut trees, just cleaned them off. Afterwards our government reimbursed them $500 for those trees. I was only making $40/month at the time. It just didn't seem right; they'd pay more for a tree than for us guys fighting the war."

Even making the meager salary that he did, Estrada made it a point to send his mother two war bonds every month.

Conditions in the Philippines were far from ideal, sometimes barely livable. Estrada remembers a typhoon lasting more than three days. "It rained so hard, we couldn't fire a shot. We were stuck in our foxholes, baling out water with our steel helmets."

Disembarking from the USS Missouri, Estrada hit the beachhead at Cebu in the Philippines. Air support covered their landing. "It was scary hearing those 16 inch shells whizzing over our heads. But my buddy gave me good advice, 'Don't worry about the ones you hear; worry about the ones you don't hear.'"

Estrada frequently felt the earth shake as rounds hit the dirt just in front of him. One bullet came a little too close for comfort, hitting the canteen he carried at his side. "That made me mad; water was mighty hard to come by over there."

But he fought on, climbing over the steep hills by zigzagging around them. Frequently his boots would slip on the slick rocks. Occasionally, he would stop and enjoy the banana trees crowding the hillsides. "I ate lots of those bananas, just like a monkey," he quipped.

After the Japanese surrendered, Estrada was shipped to Yokahama. Ray met his brother, Nick, in Tokyo before sailing for home aboard the USS Herald of the Morning. After fourteen days at sea, Estrada landed in San Francisco on Sept. 21, 1946.

After his discharge, he and his cousin were on the same bus bound for their CA. home when it broke down. Following his cousin's suggestion and lead, Estrada started hitchhiking home.

About the third or fourth guy who picked them up, suggested they stop for some pie and coffee. "He let us off to go in and order while he went across the street to fill up with gas. We never saw him or any of our stuff again," Estrada lamented. Ray felt fortunate that he carried his discharge papers and a little cash with him; his cousin lost all in the getaway car. Ray did regret losing some Japanese sabers, Philippine bolo knives, silk souvenirs for his mother, and his "lucky" bullet-hole-ridden canteen.

Finding no work near his hometown, Estrada loaded up his saddle and bedroll in his old Chevy and headed north, looking for work on cattle ranches during the summer. Ray learned "cowboying" from his father, who earned the title of "King of the Cowboys" from his peers.

Estrada worked for Ray and Kenneth Jameson in CA. When the Jamesons relocated to CO and bought the XY Ranch near Granada, they offered Estrada the general foreman position. He and his wife, Eloise, accepted and moved to Colorado. Estrada worked the XY for over thirty years before his retirement.

He claims he "retired to work." He and Eloise are constantly busy, cleaning Colorado East Bank and the offices at Granada Feeders plus taking care of sixteen yards in addition to their own.

The Estradas have five children: Ray Jr., Gloria (Martinez), Mark, Paul, and Terri (Best). They are quick to tell you their thirteen grandchildren and two great grandchildren are the real flowers of their life. "Our whole lives revolve around our grandchildren," Eloise explains as she shows off their photos.

One senses a joy of living when visiting with the Estradas, watching their warm smiles and dancing eyes as they describe their lives, work, family, and many good friends in Granada. "We couldn't be happier," they muse.

Ray serves as an example to their children and grandchildren. Their son Ray served with the U.S. Navy in Viet Nam. Carlo Best, their grandson, was a Marine. The Estrada family military tradition continues from generation to generation.

Insight: "Don't worry about the ones (bombs) you hear, worry about the ones you can't hear."

Henry Leal Guards POWs

The job of prison guard is never easy. It becomes much more difficult during time of war, guarding prisoners who do not speak your language.

Henry Leal served as a guard for Japanese POWs during World War II. When asked about the language barrier, Leal replied, "It made the job harder, but sometimes it was a blessing. They would cuss us out, and we couldn't understand a word of what they were saying."

Leal was born and raised in Lamar. In 1943 he had just gotten married and was working at the Creaghe Packing Company, when he opened his draft notice.

He went through basic training at Camp Roberts, CA. Later the Army sent him to Fort Ord, CA. then onto Fort Lewis, WA. He shipped out of Seattle, WA headed for Hawaii.

"It took us thirty days to make the trip from Seattle to Oahu, Hawaii. We spent the time zigzagging across the Pacific dodging enemy subs," Leal explained.

Leal took his jungle training on Oahu, home of Pearl Harbor. As Platoon Sergeant, he was in charge of 25 men. Their job was to guard the POWs and supervise them when they worked in the laundry.

"Those boys were pretty hard to get along with," Leal said of the POWs. "They would climb over the fences. We had to go to double guard duty to keep them in." Leal recalled one incident when one of his men had to shoot an escaping prisoner who would not be persuaded to stop his escape attempt.

Frequently, they would have to fly out to another island and bring more POWs back to Oahu. Twelve stars adorn Leal's sleeve patch, indicating the number of different islands on which he served. He was on most of the islands in the Asiatic-Pacific campaign: Hawaii, Australia, Saipan, Okinawa, and Fuji, to name just a few.

By the time of his discharge in 1946, Leal had advanced to Tech Sergeant in the Army Infantry, 27th Division, A Company.

Returning home to his wife, Eleanor, Leal finally had a chance to grieve over their infant daughter who was born after he was shipped to Hawaii and died six months later. The Army would not issue him a pass to go home to comfort his wife. He never saw his first-born child.

Leal went to work at the Lamar Custom Slaughtering Plant west of town. When that closed, he returned to work at Creaghe. Then he worked at the Lamar Housing Authority until his retirement in 1991.

He and his wife had four children: Joe, who lives in North Carolina; Stella, who lives in Englewood, CO; Connie, in Denver; and Patricia who is in Georgia. They also have five grandchildren and one great grandchild.

Leal supported the US military and the veterans who served. He was Adjutant in the Lamar Walter L. Bennett, Post 71 of the VFW.

He was also active in the Knights of Columbus, achieving the high rank of 4th Degree Knight.

When asked his view of the current war on terrorism, Leal replied, "Terrible. The world is in an uproar. We have to get after those terrorists."

No doubt some current military detainee is cussing out an American guard, who only shrugs it off because he can neither speak nor understand Arabic.

Insight: "The world is in an uproar today. We have to get after those terrorists."

Cliff DuPree Cares for Wounded Soldiers

Although married with children, Cliff DuPree saw his friends going to war and felt compelled to do his part for his country. Working at Remington Arms in Denver, DePree enlisted in the Army in 1943.

He was sent to Camp Lee near Richmond, VA for thirteen weeks of basic training. From there, he was shipped to Camp Beale, CA., near Sacramento. Here he received orders to be sent overseas. Twenty-four hours before his departure, DuPree found he would not be shipped out. No explanation given. This was the first of three different times, he had been slated to be sent overseas, but each time something or someone changed those plans.

DuPree served in several locations across the homefront. From CA, he was sent to Camp Ellis, near Peoria, IL, then onto Fitzsimmons in Denver. At Fitzsimmons, DuPree trained as a laboratory technician.

His first assignment was back to Camp Ellis, along with forty-four other troops. Unfortunately, a mix-up in orders prevented the personnel at Ellis from learning of their arrival. For two weeks, DuPree and the other guys fixed their own meals while awaiting further orders.

From there, he was sent to Camp Barkley near Abilene, TX. DuPree remembers a forced ten-mile march here. He and a buddy, Al Campbell, were leading the march. They took off their boots to soak their feet in a stream during a rest stop. DuPree remembers the blood running downstream from the sores on their feet. When they felt they could not continue, their Lieutenant encouraged them on, "Come on, you can make it. It's just over this hill." Returning from the march, their unit was quarantined in their barracks for two weeks. They never knew why.

For the second time, DuPree received overseas orders. He and 400-500 other troops were loaded on a train for the coast. Once they reached New York City; however, they discovered this was the end of the trip for them.

DuPree reached NY with less than $5 in his pocket. "I found out I didn't need anymore than that. The subway and ferry were both only five cents. If you were wearing a military uniform, you couldn't buy a meal. Someone always bought it for you."

His next assignment proved the most grueling. He was sent to New England General Hospital in Atlantic City, NJ. Here DuPree helped care for casualties from the Normandy invasion and the Battle of the Bulge. It broke his heart and spirit to see so many men paralyzed or suffering amputations.

Leaving Atlantic City, DuPree moved on to Camp Crowder, MO. He had pleasant memories of discovering some wild strawberry patches here during his time on the rifle range.

At one point, DuPree volunteered to be sent to China where troops would parachute from planes trying to locate General Stillwell. The Army did not want to send him on that assignment because he was married, and they needed him in the hospitals here at home.

His next assignment was at Camp McCain near Granada, MS. Here he worked with 300-400 German prisoners from Rommel's campaign through North Africa. They had malaria. Among his other responsibilities, DuPree drew their blood for daily hemotology tests.

His last assignment was back at Camp Crowder.

DuPree was discharged on Nov. 11, 1945 from Company A of the 28th Training Battalion.

After his discharge, DuPree joined his wife and children who had moved to Holly, CO., to be with her folks. Two of their children, Brook and Gary were born before he enlisted. Mark was born in June, 1945, shortly before his discharge from the Army. Their daughter, Maris, was born after he returned home.

DuPree worked for Romer Young in Holly for thirty-eight years before his retirement.

Some soldiers fought their way through South Pacific jungles or foxholes in Europe. Cliff DuPree of Holly quietly served in hospital wards across America caring for wounded soldiers.

Upon his enlistment, Cliff DuPree received an unusual pocket-sized Bible with a metal cover. Inside the cover was this message from President Franklin D. Roosevelt.

As Commander-in-Chief, I take pleasure in commending the reading of the Bible to all who serve in the armed forces of the United States. Throughout the centuries men of many faiths and diverse origins have found in the Sacred Book words of wisdom, counsel, and inspiration. It is a fountain of strength and, now, as always, an aid in attaining the highest aspirations of the human soul.

"Bibles like that have literally saved lives of several soldiers," DuPree recounted. "That metal cover deflected bullets that would've killed those guys."

Insight: "They also serve, who serve at home."

Bob Lubbers Invades Okinawa with the Marines

He stands by the sanctuary door shaking hands and greeting churchgoers in a quiet and unassuming manner. One would not necessarily associate this image of Bob (Robert) Lubbers with a former tough Marine who invaded both Okinawa and Tokyo harbor during World War II and then went on to become an accomplished scuba diver. Facing a rewarding future, Bob Lubbers tells of a remarkable past.

Interrupting his studies at Colorado State University School of Veterinary Medicine, Lubbers returned home to Wiley to help his father, Otto Lubbers (a World War I veteran), finish the fall farm work before enlisting in the Marines in December 1943. He recalls spending Christmas Day at the Marine Corp depot in San Diego.

He taught new recruits at Camp Pendleton such basic skills as rope tying, airplane identification, and gas mask training. He continued his own training at Guadalcanal in the Solomon Islands, learning jungle survival skills.

"One of the first things I learned was to keep my arms away from the mosquito netting and to shake out the sheets and my shoes (for lizards)," Lubbers commented. Then with a sly smile added, "Of course, I also learned that my mattress cover made a great makeshift surf board."

Lubbers and his outfit, the 6th Marine Division, 4th Regiment, 2nd Battalion, supported the invasion of Okinawa. Lubbers hit the beaches of Okinawa with the 11th wave of invaders during Operation Iceberg, the military term for the invasion of the Ryukyus, on Easter Sunday, April 1, 1945. "We sustained very few casualties and met with little opposition initially," remembers

Lubbers. That soon changed as the Japanese risked everything they had in order to defend Okinawa.

A reported 60,000 Japanese troops and 100,000 Okinawan guardsmen were hiding on the island ready to thwart the invaders. In addition, 1465 Kamikazes pounded the Navy ships, which ringed the island.

Lubbers headed north with the 6th Marines and engaged in fierce battle on the Motobu Peninsula.

As Communications Wireman, Lubbers served close to the action. He installed the telephone line so the forward observer could communicate with the 81mm mortars. "I laid miles and miles of wire," Lubber explained. "I worked to keep it out of the roadways so the tanks and trucks wouldn't tear it down.

"I timed my advances right before dark. Frequently the Japanese fired mortar rounds directed at me. Fortunately, it typically landed behind me. I ran to keep ahead of it. A friend tried to cover me with his machine gun fire.

"The Japanese designed ambushes by putting pins in the wire. As we ran along fingering the wire trying to find the problem with the message transmission, they would jump us. Consequently, we avoided working during dark of night."

Lubbers and his outfit frequently encountered sniper fire. Near Naha a sniper attacked as they were going over a sea wall. Later as they crossed a footbridge, their commander barked, "Hurry up, this sniper is trying to fire at every 4th guy." Fortunately, their unit made it across without fatalities.

One of their main battles, cited as one of the turning points of the invasion, occurred at a castle near Shuri, the ancient capitol of Okinawa east of Naha. The Marines were taking a beating from enemy fire coming from the hills surrounding the castle. "Company C turned the Japs own ingenuity against them by moving assault elements through the tunnel system the enemy had dug underneath the castle and succeeded in getting behind the Japs," explained Lubbers. "We were soon able to overtake them."

Lubbers spent 101 days on Okinawa before leaving on the 21st of June 1945. President Truman awarded the Presidential Unit Citation to the Sixth Marine Division for "extraordinary heroism in action against enemy Japanese forces during the assault and capture of Okinawa."

From there, Lubbers was sent to Guam. "An interesting sidelight," Lubbers adds, "I was on Guam when I spotted two of my cousins, Lloyd and Floyd Lubbers. I also saw Ed Lay, my college roommate. Later on a ship bound for Japan, I saw Freddie Betz."

Following a short stop in Guam, Lubbers shipped out to Japan. He was part of the "new" 4th Marine regiment deployed to liberate members of the "old" 4th Marines captured in the Philippines. Lubbers and a group of other Marines provided a defensive perimeter for the demolition crew, which went in and "spiked" (rendered inoperable) the enemy's guns around Tokyo Bay.

"Then we loaded up and went to mainland Japan," Lubbers explained. "I was one of the first guys in." There he served as a switchboard operator.

"Truman is my hero," declared Lubbers. "He dropped the bomb, ending the war. I was slated to be part of the outfit to invade the Tokyo plain in October. I probably would've been killed in that maneuver."

Discharged May 5, 1946, Lubbers went back to farming. "I just didn't want to be around crowds of people."

Bob Lubbers married and had three children, Cindy, Connie, and Curtis and four grandsons, Curtis II, Clay, Chris, and Chad.

He became a successful farmer, earning several awards in the process. Including, among others, the 1988 Conservationist of the Year for Prowers County and FFA Chapter Farmer.

During several summers his grandson, Curtis II, came and helped him farm. Clay and his new bride (to be married in April) will be moving into the house vacated by Bob. So the cycle of the family farm continues through another generation.

His story does not end there. Lubbers traveled throughout the United States and around the world on several farm tours. Including his war time presence in Japan, Lubbers has been on all seven continents of the world.

In South America, Lubbers visited farms in Argentina, much like the ones here. He canoed into the interior of Brazil looking for "small alligators" (less than 2 inches between their eyes).

He attended a farm machinery show in Paris exhibiting John Deere and New Holland equipment. Elsewhere in Europe, Lubbers traveled to Switzerland, Germany, and England.

Along the Gold Coast of Australia, he discovered large wheat farms similar to the ones in Southeast Colorado. He visited New Zealand sheep ranches.

In Kenya, Africa, Lubbers talked with members of the Masai tribe. "They claimed to own all the cattle in the world. They just haven't gotten them all gathered up yet," Lubbers quipped.

Venturing to the far southern tip of our planet, Lubbers enjoyed seeing the icebergs and penguins in Antarctica.

Inspired by the beautiful seashells he found at Guadalcanal, Lubbers took up scuba diving, logging 75 deep-sea dives from the Red Sea to the Philippines. He learned to dive in the Cayman Islands. "We hand fed the sting rays found in the shallows where fishermen cleaned their catch."

Egypt was the stepping off shore for his Red Sea dives. He described seeing beautiful coral walls. Elsewhere in Egypt, he toured Luxor, the Valley of the Kings, and the Pyramids near Cairo.

He swam with the sharks in the Palau Islands, southwest of Guam, and the whales in the Sea of Cortez.

Lubbers enjoyed snorkeling in the Galapagos Islands. "The seals like to play with us divers. You could feel them gliding over your shoulders," he described. "There were thousands of turtles there.

"One of the highlights of my travels was watching the leatherhead turtles lay their eggs at midnight off the coast of Costa Rica--sometimes as many as 50 eggs at one time. We were able to see a few hatch and swim out to sea."

Other memorable dives occurred near the Roatan Island, off the coast of Honduras—the Barrier Reef makes for spectacular diving; Yap Island-- he watched giant manta rays; the Blue Hole in Belize--Jacques Cousteau worked there; and Truk Island-- the American Navy sank several Japanese ships, which rest on the bottom of the sea.

When asked to name his favorite dive, he replied, "The one I'm going on next."

His travels are documented with several amazing photographs he took and has displayed in his home. Among them are an African elephant, whales, a lobster, sea turtles, icebergs, and cheetahs. All of which are National Geographic quality.

Although Bob Lubbers has visited many places and experienced the best and worst of humanity, his value system stands solidly on home and family. It can best be illustrated with a story he related. "In Costa Rica, I was visiting with Ed, an engineer who worked on the World Trade Center Towers in New York City. He commented I must be the richest man in Colorado. I agreed. Being able to farm and spend time with my grandsons makes me feel like the richest man in Colorado.

Insight: "Being able to farm and spend time with my grandson makes me feel like the richest man in Colorado."

George Frank Uses Horse Sense to Serve in War

As a young man, George Frank, helped his father raise and train Arabian horses on their ranch southwest of Scottsdale, Arizona. In the spring of 1941, George accompanied a businessman back to Ohio. While there, he was inducted into the U.S. Army on his 25th birthday.

Frank was sent to Ft. Warren (now Warren Air Force base) in Cheyenne, Wyoming, to begin his basic training in October. Then December 7, 1941 happened.

Frank and other soldiers with an agricultural or livestock background were shipped to Ft. Bliss, Texas, to become Troop B of the 252 Quartermaster Remount Troop to assist the First Cavalry division. Their job was to furnish pack animals, including horses and mules, for General Stillwell's army. Stillwell was training the Chinese to rout the Japanese out of India.

Frank was onboard the Samuel H. Walker Liberty ship when it left the U.S. in 1944 with a load of mules. Traveling at the speed of 9 knots, it took them over 30 days to reach their destination in Calcutta, India. Once they docked, General Stillwell came onboard, shook hands with the troops and instructed them to bring more pack animals.

This time they went to New Caladonia and returned with Australian horses. Frank assisted with a total of three shiploads of pack animals, 350 animals each trip.

Once they landed in Calcutta, they would load the animals onto rail cars and take them to the end of the rail line near Ledo, India. From there, Frank and the other soldiers would take the horses into Burma, over the unfinished Burma Road. This was a sixteen-day trip over mountainous terrain, with the soldiers each riding one animal and leading another. They would then return by plane and begin another mission, riding and leading the horses.

On one particular trip, Frank related they had smuggled some S & W coffee off the ship to enjoy on those cold mornings on horseback. Just as they were brewing their last pot over an open fire, Japanese planes approached. Regretfully, they had to douse the flames with the last drops of their coveted brew.

It was not all work and no play as Frank's outfit of soldiers/cowboys enjoyed impromptu rodeos almost on a daily basis.

"I wouldn't take a million dollars for my Army time," Frank said in summary and then added, "neither would I repeat it for a million."

Frank was discharged from the Army in February, 1946. "I was eligible for discharge earlier, but there were still horses in northern India someone had to care for.

Frank returned to Scottsdale to help his father raise and train Arabian horses. Much to Frank's dismay, the "urban sprawl" of Phoenix was rapidly encroaching on their territory.

So when the opportunity came to visit his cousin, Earl Labertew of Lamar, CO., who had come to Arizona to purchase horses and then returned to Colorado, Frank did not hesitate. He liked the small town atmosphere of Lamar.

When the First National Bank president offered Frank a job as record keeper and teller, he accepted and kept the job for 32 years. "I never applied for a job in my life," Frank quipped.

Frank received his bank teller's training from E. Lundgren. During the infamous Fleagle gang bank robbery in Lamar, they shoved Lundgren out of their getaway car, fearing he might be too recognizable with only one arm.

Frank's knowledge of horses was invaluable to the war effort, and his love of horses is still obvious. He and his wife, Eleanor, have several paintings of horses in their home and many ceramic horse figurines in their backyard studio, Kay's Clay Palace.

Insight: "I wouldn't take a million dollars for my Army time. Neither would I repeat if for a million."

James Hanagan Travels Around the World

"I am proud to say I traveled completely around the world in the service of my country," James Hanagan reminisced.

"After high school, I attended college for a year. That was back in 1932-33. My father and uncle farmed 120 acres of prime farmland near Swink. Farming was in my blood; I just had to get back to the land."

"Later when I was working for the War Department in Salt Lake City, Utah, I decided I wanted to be closer to home. My wife, Velma, is also from this area, having grown up near Rocky Ford."

He was able to get a transfer to Camp Amache, near Granada, CO.

Two weeks before he was to be drafted, James enlisted in the engineering branch of the Army. "I'd carried a shovel over my shoulder farming, and I decided I didn't want to spend my time in the military carrying a rifle over my shoulder."

When he left for basic training in Camp Claiborne, Louisiana, near Alexandria, he felt like, "How lucky can a guy get, being sent south for the winter'?" James recollected. "Boy, was I wrong. I nearly froze to death, crawling on my belly in ice water with bullets whizzing over my head during assault training. It was a miserable time."

"After basic training, I interviewed for Officer Candidate School (OCS) and was assigned to Fort Belvoir, Virginia."

"It was an intensive 17 weeks. Since I was nearly thirty years old, I had to learn to study all over again. But knowing I had to do my best for my wife and daughter back home, I learned to bark out orders like an officer."

After OCS, James was sent back to Camp Claiborne where he was assigned to a battalion of African Americans. They shipped out of West Palm Beach, Florida to Ledo, India. From there, they convoyed to northern Burma, near Myitkyina.

As members of the 1327 Engineering Regiment, James' troop assignment was to build a warehouse over 1200 feet long, billets or barracks, and a mess hall. This entailed opening up a gravel pit and building a segment of road, a portion of the Ledo-Burma Road.

James was in charge of finding and caring for "haylong" trees, a wood similar to mahogany. The termites would eat all other kinds of wood but this.

After the warehouse was built, they maintained the road. The troops had a bit more free time, during which they enjoyed fishing in a nearby river. Their method was a bit unorthodox. They would drop quarter pound blocks of explosives into the water and capture the fish that rose to the surface. One day they caught a catfish large enough to feed a whole company of men.

Another responsibility Lt. Hanagan had was flying to Myitkyina to pick up the company payroll, which was issued in rupees. "I didn't sleep well with the money under my pillow and a .45 strapped on my hip."

Although not in direct combat, James fought the elements of nature, from malaria-carrying mosquitoes to monsoon rains to tigers.

One night a tiger entered a six-man tent, while the soldiers slept. Following his tracks, the soldiers could see where the tiger went around each man before attacking the last man in the tent.

Maintaining the road during monsoon season was a challenge. It would rain over 300 inches a year from mid-May to October. "We'd use French drains to help divert the water coming down out of the mountains, as we had no culverts. After a torrential rain of thirty inches one night, trees piled up against a Bailey bridge. We had to use TNT to blast them away, destroying the bridge. Then it was necessary to quickly rebuild a heavy pontoon bridge for the convoy carrying equipment. I worked over forty hours straight that time." James received his silver bar, marking his promotion to First Lieutenant.

"When the war was over, I called Velma and told her I was coming home. But the next day I was sent to Shanghai to act as a liaison between the Nationalist and Communist Chinese under the Marshall Plan.

He was then shipped to Camp Maryville, near Oakland, California, where he received hishonorable discharge. In October 1946 he completed his trip around the world when he rode the train from California back to Lamar.

Velma and James were blessed with two more daughters, Joyce and Joan.

Joan, the youngest, is a RN and PA married to Dr. Marc Sindler, who received the honor of being named "Colorado Family Practitioner of 2000." They live in Canon City, CO., and have twelve-year old twins, a boy and a girl.

Joyce, a music teacher is living in Colorado Springs with her daughter.

Jane lives in Pueblo, CO., where she worked in the state hospital as a RN with a Masters degree in Behavioral Science. She has three children, the oldest daughter is a lawyer and the two younger sons are both RNs.

After traveling around the world, serving in World War II, James Hanagan chose to raise his family -- and lots of vegetables--in Lamar, Colorado.

Insight: "When farming is in your blood, you just have to get back to the land."

Willy Bridge Helps Refuel the Enola Gay

December 7, 1941, Willy Bridge, living in San Diego, CA., learns of the attack on Pearl Harbor. Residents in San Diego watch their skies in alarm, fearful the Japanese would move their attack inland; San Diego being a prime location for such an attack because of the large military base there. Fortunately, such an attack did not occur.

January 4, 1943, Willy Bridge was inducted into the Army. He was sent to St. Petersburg, FL., for basic training. "It was so cold there, I nearly froze to death," Bridge describes.

From there, Bridge was sent to Chanute Field, Illinois and onto Hays, KA, where he was assigned to the Army Air Corp at Liberal, KA. Liberal was the B24 training base for new pilots flying four engines planes. Bridge was one of the first troops sent there after its creation. He became part of the crash crew who cleaned up the aircraft debris after crashes. He remembers one devastating mid-air crash at Liberal, "There were about 9 or 10 crew members in each plane."

On Easter Sunday, a short while after he arrived at Liberal, Bridge describes a tornado touching down on the base, "It took a barracks and a warehouse, fortunately, it skipped over our barracks." Growing up in San Diego, Bridge had never experienced a tornado.

While in Liberal, Bridge became acquainted with several of the local folks. One young lady in particular, Pauline Petersen, took his fancy. They were married on Oct. 30, 1943. Pauline had grown up near Two Buttes, CO., and was working in Liberal, KS., at the time.

Bridge was sent to San Francisco then onto Hickam Field in Honolulu. He was assigned to the Army Transport Command (ATC). They transported troops to Saipan and brought back the wounded on C54, 4-engine, transport planes.

Bridge's 17-member ATC outfit was sent to Kwajalein in the Marshall Islands. There they served as the crash crew and helped with refueling planes.

"I was on that island fourteen months. It was one mile wide and three miles long. I felt like a prisoner on that island," quips Bridge.

They sent Bridge to Hawaii for a short R & R. He met and became friends with Hilo Hattie, a Hawaiian entertainer who sang with the Royal Hawaiian Band.

It was a hot, sultry day in mid-July on Kwajalein Island when two B29s stopped in for refueling. The ATC members wondered at the tight security surrounding the planes. Bridge met the pilot of one of the planes, Col. Paul W. Tibbets, who flew the Enola Gay. They were on their way to Tinian Island, a small island in the Marianas. Less than a month later, on Aug. 6, 1945, The Enola Gay carried the first atom bomb that was dropped on Japan, ending the war. Bridge learned later the second plane that landed on Kwajalein that day carried the detonator for the atomic bomb.

On his birthday, Sept. 23 of that same year, 1945, Bridge was sent back to the States, to Letterman Hospital in San Francisco. He met his first-born son, Randy, for the first time in San Francisco. Randy was sixteen months old by then. Bridge had been in the middle of the ocean when his son was born. Randy grew up to become a paratrooper in Panama during the days of the Viet Nam Conflict.

In Nov. 1945, Bridge traveled to Washington for his discharge.

He recalls his mother saving a pineapple for his welcome home meal. Pineapple had been a favorite of his before his military days. "But that pineapple didn't look very good to me. They fixed pineapple (in the Pacific) every which way: fried, boiled, or steamed. I was tired of pineapple by then," he laughs.

Bringing Pauline back to her home area, Bridge settled in Lamar, working in the light plant and selling automobiles until his retirement. For the last 25 years during the summer, he has helped Al Tinnes out as a member of the ground crew.

grandchildren. One of their favorite pastimes is receiving emails and photos from their grandchildren who live all over the US.

When Willy Bridge's grandchildren and great grandchildren are old enough to understand, I hope he will share with them the story of the day he helped Paul Tibbets refuel the Enola Gay.

Insight: "You never know when some routine job you do will become history in the making."

Howard Herbaugh Moves Men and Machines

His office was the interior of a 2.5-ton Jimmy truck. His responsibility was to transport men and supplies from the company command post to the front lines and back again to military headquarters.

Tech Corporal Howard Herbaugh was assigned to the motor pool with the 230th Signal Operations Company attached to several different units during World War II. They helped out wherever the need was the greatest.

Herbaugh had just begun his job at the Pueblo Ordinance Depot as Jr. Operating Engineer copying blueprints onto paper when he was called to serve his country in 1943.

Reporting to Ft. Logan, Herbaugh was sent to Ft. Bend, Oregon, with the Corps of Engineers.

During Basic Training, Herbaugh reported learning how to march, handle firearms, and standard operating procedures for general Army duty. However, his most memorable lesson involved learning how to make a "good" cup of coffee. He was working in the kitchen one morning when the cook ordered him to make the coffee. "Having never done it before, I made what I thought was coffee," Herbaugh explained. "My parents never drank coffee, whether or not they didn't like the taste of it or couldn't afford it, I don't know. Anyway, the soldiers and officers started complaining about my coffee that morning."

When the Sergeant found out from the cook Herbaugh had made the coffee, he asked, "What is this stuff, hot water or weak tea? Whatever it is, it's not fit to wash your feet in. Don't you know a soldier's breakfast is a cup of good coffee and a cigarette? I'll show you how to make coffee."

After those encouraging words, the Sergeant proceeded to instruct Herbaugh to run the water through the grounds at least six times. "A good cup of coffee will look like maple syrup," he described. From then on, Herbaugh made his coffee thick and black.

After Basic, Herbaugh was sent to PA for six weeks of advanced training, "We learned how to crawl on our bellies through a snow tunnel." Herbaugh questioned the merit of that training when he learned he would be serving in the South Pacific.

For forty-two days, Herbaugh's outfit zigzagged across the Pacific in a made-over Italian luxury liner, the U.S.S. Hermitage, along with 10,000 other soldiers and 1500 sailors plus officers and crew.

The luxury accommodations were the part "made over." "I had to wait two weeks just to get a shower," Herbaugh recalls. "They'd turn the soft water on for two hours in the morning and two hours in the afternoon. Once I got to the head of the line just to be told the water was off. Another time I got all soaped up and they shut the water off before I could rinse."

Herbaugh initially served in the jungles of southern New Guinea. "Nothing stinks as bad as a swampy jungle," he recalled.

From there, he was sent to Luzon in the Philippines to train for the invasion of Japan, predicted to take place around Oct. '45. Because of fierce national loyalty, the Japanese civilians were expected to be as big a threat as the military. Experts predicted over a million and a half casualties from that invasion, which fortunately never took place.

While not being in the thick of the battle, their motor pool frequently sustained sniper attacks. Other times they would have surprise visitors. "Every once in awhile," Herbaugh reported, "we'd have a stranger in our chow line. A stranded Japanese soldier, separated from his company and facing starvation would surrender to our chow line and the waiting MP's."

Herbaugh remembers the night the war officially ended. He was pulling guard duty on the north end of their compound. "We'd been having trouble with nationals stealing our clothing. Some of the guys went into a nearby village. It started to rain, monsoon-like, while they were gone. They returned shortly, whooping it up and shouting something about the Japs had surrendered. I figured they had a little too much to drink to know what was really going on. But, pretty soon, some other guys, sober this time, came by and said, 'Hey guard, the war is ended. Japan surrendered!'

"I thought to myself, 'What am I doing standing out here in the rain for then?' I headed inside."

Herbaugh served in Yokahama, Japan from Sept. 1945 to Feb. 1946. He described total desolation of the Japanese countryside and starving women who took handfuls of garbage from dumpsters and fed it to the children wrapped on their backs. He and other American G.I's would stow extra food away on their trays and give it to the starving children.

When the American government started giving food rations to the Japanese people, it was not unusual to see bodies frozen to death waiting outside overnight for a few morsels of food.

After his discharge, Herbaugh returned to Pueblo. The Ordinance Depot was downsizing and laying off employees. The job, which they promised to hold for him, was eliminated. Herbaugh went to work for a dry cleaning business.

Some friends at church introduced Howard to Dorothy Hood, who was living in Lamar. "It took us over two years to tie the knot, but it has stayed tied now for over 50 years." Dorothy and Howard were married June 6, 1951.

In 1952, they moved to Lamar, where he worked in the Sprout and then the Smith Cleaners until his retirement. He and Dorothy had two children. Their oldest, Sharon, worked for the Associated Press and was killed in a helicopter accident in Afghanistan several years ago. They raised her daughter, Tracie, who studied Journalism at the University of Colorado. Their son,

Marlin, is an EMT working for Prowers Medical Center in Lamar in the Emergency Room and with the Lamar Fire Department.

Howard enjoys working in his yard and collecting miniature cars. "Mostly I like old Model A's and Model T's, old trucks, ones I can relate to from my youth," Howard explains.

I'm sure if you stopped by for a visit, Howard would sit and chat a bit, show you his flowering shrubs, and brew you a "good" cup of coffee.

Insight: "A good cup of coffee is like maple syrup—thick and black."

George Allen with The Tokyo Force Leads the Convoy to Japanese Surrender

George Allen joined the Navy in 1943. Living on a ranch south of Holly, CO., he had never heard of places like Leyta Gulf and Surigao Strait. During the following three years, however, he sailed through these areas and many other strange-sounding places in the South Pacific, eventually sailing into Tokyo Bay for the Japanese surrender.

Initially, he was stationed at Farragut, Idaho. Then he attended radio school in San Diego, CA, before being assigned to the U.S.S. Mt. Olympus, a communications ship.

As part of the Third Amphibious Force, later known as The Tokyo Force, Allen operated the radios onboard ship. "Six or eight of us would work the radios," Allen recalls. "Sitting around a horseshoe-shaped table in front of us, a group of officers, Navy pilots, would listen to the radio calls. We picked up both Army and Navy signals."

Times and places tended to run together as Allen sailed throughout the South Pacific. Some of the names he remembers include: Mindoro Sea, South China Sea, Sulu Sea, Surigao Strait, Sogod Bay, Lingayan Gulf. They monitored the fighting in the Philippines, Solomon Islands, Palau Islands, New Guinea, and others.

During the Palau invasion, Allen's ship was sailing in the Luzian Gulf when they spotted a plane coming right at them. At the last minute, the plane veered and fired on the U.S.S. Pennsylvania right behind them.

Allen remembers crossing the equator in the Leyte Gulf on Sept. 30, 1944.

Their ship took a hit near Yap Island. With the ship listing and sailing ten feet below the water line, they headed for the Philippines. While docked, the ship was raised above the water and the crew was sent overboard to scrape barnacles off the hull.

With no bathing available on board, the crew looked forward to swimming around in those warm waters. "We jumped off that bow, which was about 40 feet above the water," Allen describes. "Soon we found ourselves swimming in waters full of barracudas and sharks."

When their outfit received orders to make project models of the South Pacific islands, Allen and E.L.Smith were selected for the job. They made plaster casts of the islands.

Allen's ship led the convoy into Tokyo Bay. The U.S.S. Missouri tied up side by side to the U.S.S. Mt. Olympus, commanded by Admiral Byrd and Admiral Wilkinson.

"I'll never forget that sight," recalls Allen. "The bay was circled with mountains. We could see the Japanese gun mounts all painted white (indicating surrender) and the bodies of dead Japanese soldiers still floating in the water.

"The first day we just sat there. On the second and third days, they took us, 25 guys at a time, on a tour of Yokohama.

On their way out of Japan, they battled a typhoon near northern Honshu. "Our bow went under water many times fighting that storm."

They stopped for R & R in Hawaii. Arriving back in the States in 1946, Allen first went to his sister's in Ft. Morgan, CO. Then he headed to Holly to work the wheat harvest. Eventually he was headed to Kansas. In his words, "I was headed to Oz, when I stopped at the Shell station in Holly to work for sixty cents an hour." He continued his employment there for nineteen and a half years.

In 1947, Allen married Myrtle Parker. They had four children: Jeanne, who died when she was seven years old; John, who farms near Holly; Sherry, living in New Mexico; and Susie, who works in West Virginia as a traveling nurse. Myrt, as George affectionately called her, died in 1968. He has six grandchildren and nine great grandchildren.

Allen lives south of Holly near the area he grew up. As he scans the photo album he put together after the war, those strange-sounding names of the South Pacific are a distant memory. The contribution Allen made as part of The Tokyo Force, however, looms large on the warfront horizon.

Shown here is one of the photos in George Allen's album taken during the Japanese surrender. Pictured are General McArthur and Nimitz of the Allied powers and the Emperor of Japan. Courtesy photo

Insight: "Sometimes the best and only bath available is in water shared by barracudas and sharks."

History of Veterans Day

In 1921, an unknown World War I American soldier was buried in Arlington National Cemetery. Similar ceremonies occurred earlier in England and France, where an unknown soldier was buried in each nation's highest place of honor (in England, Westminster Abbey; in France, the Arc de Triomphe). These memorial gestures all took place on November 11, giving universal recognition to the celebrated ending of World War I fighting at 11 a.m., November 11, 1918 (the 11th hour of the 11th day of the 11th month). The day became known as "Armistice Day."

Armistice Day officially received its name in America in 1926 through a Congressional resolution. It became a national holiday 12 years later by similar Congressional action. If the idealistic hope had been realized that World War I was "the War to end all wars," November 11 might still be called Armistice Day. But only a few years after the holiday was proclaimed, war broke out in Europe. Sixteen and one-half million Americans took part. Four hundred seven thousand of them died in service, more than 292,000 in battle.

An answer to the question of how to pay tribute to those who had served in this latest, great war came in a proposal made by Representative Edwin K. Rees of Kansas: Change Armistice Day to Veterans Day, and make it an occasion to honor those who have served America in all wars. In 1954 President Eisenhower signed a bill proclaiming November 11 as Veterans Day.

Looking Back- Lessons in Liberty

We flip a light switch and the lights come on; we drive to the gas station and there is gas and we can afford it; we cross a border from one state to the next, and we show no identification card or passport; we turn on the radio or the television and can freely and immediately access hundreds of channels of broad-ranging, multi-dimensional information, commentary, and music; we can publicly disagree with our leaders; we can worship where and when the Spirit so moves us; and we can choose our friends from among a myriad of cultures, faith, creeds, and skin colors.

We can do all these things and so much more because our grandparents, our parents, our brothers, sisters, aunts, uncles, and friends in uniform made a commitment to America.

Each year as we observe Veterans Day, let us pay tribute to the heroes of yesterday with thanksgiving and prayer and rededicate ourselves to the cause of peace without fear.

As America strikes back, escalating the war on terrorism, the words of President Dwight D. Eisenhower are as significant today as when he uttered them in 1954 proclaiming Nov. 11 as the official Veterans Day, "Let us solemnly remember the sacrifices of all those who fought so valiantly, on the seas, in the air, and on foreign shores, to preserve our heritage of freedom, and let us reconsecrate ourselves to the task of promoting an enduring peace so that their efforts shall not have been in vain."

Memorial Day- Background of the Holiday

Memorial Day-- time for family outings and backyard barbecues, the first long weekend of summer. Hopefully, this year we will pause to remember the significance of the holiday.

On Memorial Day let us give thanks that we live in a free nation and give thanks for all those who served that we might enjoy the blessings of liberty.

Memorial Day was originally called Decoration Day. Organized women's groups in the South were decorating graves before the end of the Civil War.

While Waterloo N.Y. was officially declared the birthplace of Memorial Day by President Lyndon Johnson in May 1966, it's difficult to prove the origins of the day. It is more likely that it had many separate beginnings.

Memorial Day was officially proclaimed on May 5, 1868 by General John Logan, national commander of the Grand Army of the Republic, and was first observed on May 30, 1868 at Belle Island, a burial ground for Union soldiers near Richmond, Virginia. The mayor and the school superintendent planned the program of speeches and hymns and had the graves decorated with flowers.

The date of May 30 was attributed to a Virginian of French descent, Cassandra Oliver Moncure, who may have chosen that date because it is the "The Day of Ashes" in France when Napolean's remains were brought back to France from St. Helena.

It is now celebrated in almost every state on the last Monday in May. This date was made a federal holiday in 1971. In 1999 bills were introduced into the House and Senate to return the observance of Memorial Day to May 30th. The bills were referred to the Committee on the Judiciary and the Committee on Government Reform. To date, there have been no further developments on the bill.

Several southern states have an additional, separate day for honoring the Confederate war dead: January 19 in Texas (Robert E. Lee's birthday), April 26 in Alabama, Florida, Georgia, and Mississippi; May 10 in South Carolina; and June 3 (Jefferson Davis' birthday) in Louisiana and Tennessee.

Since the late 50's, on the Thursday before Memorial Day, the 1200 soldiers of the 3rd U.S. Infantry place small American flags at each of the more than 260,000 gravestones at Arlington

National Cemetery. They then patrol 24 hours a day during the weekend to ensure that each flag remains standing.

Since World War I, it has also been called Poppy Day. Volunteers sell little red, artificial flowers as a fund- raiser for disabled veterans. In 1915, Moina Michael conceived of the idea of wearing red poppies on Memorial Day in honor of those who died serving the nation during war. She was the first to wear one, and sold poppies to her friends and co-workers with the money going to benefit servicemen in need. Later a Madam Guerin from France was visiting the United States and learned of this new custom. When she returned to France, she made artificial red poppies to raise money for the war-orphaned children and widowed women. This tradition spread to other countries.

Many Americans have forgotten the meaning and tradition of Memorial Day. To help Americans remember the meaning of the day, the National Moment of Remembrance resolution was passed in Dec. 2000 which asks that at 3 p.m. local time, for all Americans "To voluntarily and informally observe in their own way a 'Moment of Remembrance and Respect', pausing from whatever they are doing for a moment of silence or listening to 'Taps' ".

"Taps" originated in July 1862, after the Seven Days battles at Harrison's Landing near Richmond, Virginia. A wounded Commander in the Army of the Potomac, General Daniel Butterfield, reworked another bugle call, "Scott Tattoo," with his bugler, Oliver Wilcox Norton, to create Taps. He thought that the regular call for Lights Out was too formal. The custom, thus originated, was taken up throughout the Army of the Potomac. Soon other Union units began using Taps, as did a few Confederate units. After the war, Taps became an official bugle call.

Taps was first used at a military funeral during the Peninsular Campaign in 1862. A soldier of Tidball's Battery A of the 2nd Artillery was buried at a time when the battery occupied an advanced position concealed in the woods. It was unsafe to fire the customary three volleys over the grave, on account of the proximity of the enemy, and it occurred to Capt. Tidball that the sounding of Taps would be the most appropriate ceremony that could be substituted.

There are no "official" words to Taps. The most popular are:

"Day is done, gone the sun, From the hills, from the lake, From the
skies. All is well, safely rest, God is nigh.
Go to sleep, peaceful sleep, May the soldier or sailor, God keep.
On the land or the deep, Safe in sleep.
Love, good night, Must thou go, When the day, And the night
Need thee so? All is well. Speedeth all To their rest.
Fates the light; And afar Goeth day, And the stars Shineth bright,
Fare the well; Day has gone, Night is on.
Thanks and praise, For our days, 'Neath the sun, 'Neath the stars,
  'Neath the sky, As we go, This we know, God is nigh."

PROWERS COUNTY VETERANS WHO GAVE ALL

Following is a list of Prowers County Military personnel who lost their lives in WWI, WWII, the Korean Conflict or Vietnam. Their names are recorded on the Prowers County Memorial Monument.

World War I

BARNHART, Corney J.
BENNETT, Walter L.
BEWLEY, Jesse A.
CONRAD, Burr Murray
COOPER, John C.
CREAGHE, Saint George
DAVIS, Aaron R.
DUNN, Robert T.
FOSTER, Alfred E.
GOODMAN, Benedict H.C.
HOVEY, Robert L.
KEENE, Herdie E.
KERR, Wilber M.
MARTIN, Eric C.
MINDER, Ray
MOLL, Henry Laird
NEWSON, Ora R.
NEWMAN, Floyd L.
PARADEIS, Leonard
PRIOR, Burt A. M.
ROCKWELL, Merl
TRUJILLO, Jose E
VAGHER, Emiel H.

World War II

AKIMOTO, John
AKIMOTO, Victor
ALLENBAUGH, Orville L.
BAILEY, Roy H.
BAKER, Paul Leon
BARNES, Clifford O.
BARRIOS, Valentin G.
BIRD, Paul H.
BLEVENS, Frank E.
BRYANT, Virgil V.
CAMPBELL, Kendall C.
CARR, Millard L.
MITCHELL, Felix G.
MOORE, Lloyd F.
MORGAN, Edward M.
MORIGUCHI, Haruto
MORIHARA, Akira
MORSE, Francis J.
MORSE, Norman R.
MOURER, Ralph L.
MURANAGA, Kiyoshi .
NAKAGAKI, Masao
NAKAMURA, Ned
NEAL, Carson E.

CASTRO, Adelaido
CLORE, Norman M.
CORBETT, James J.
CROFT, Cleo G.
CROSS, Johnny
DAVIS, Walter E.
DONEY, Wesley
DUNCAN, Ellsworth
ELSWICK, Walter E.
FERGUSON, Albert F.
FISHER, Clifford W.
GIDEON, Elmer M.
GOODMAN, Frederick L.
GRIBBEN, Kenneth
HARMAN, Elmer L. Jr.
HATTORI, Kunio
HEADDING, Arthur S.
HORN, Carl D.
INOUYE, Chikara
KAMMARCAL, Harold H.
KANDA, Frank T.
KARATSU, J. Saburo
KAWAMOTO, Haruo
KENNARD, Omer E.
KERR, Ivan H.
KIKUCHI, Leo
KIMURA, John S.
KINOSHITA, Mamoru
LARRICK, James H.
MARSH, George L.
MASUDA, Elzo
MASUOKA, Peter S.
McCALL, Howard C.
McCORKLE, John P.
McEWEN, Roy A.
MENDOZA, Jess
MILLER, Clarence E. Jr.
MILLER, Leonard R.

NOE, Bruce H.
OHKI, Arnold
OKIDA, Katsunoshin
ONOUYE, Lloyd M.
OROZCO, Carlos
POSEY, Jack B.
PRICE, Carlos E.
RALSTON, Ferrol D.
RALSTON, Wilbur L.
SAITO, Calvin T.
SAITO, George S.
SAKAMOTO, Masami
SALDANA, Lawrence T.
SCHWARTZ, Albert R.
SEARS, Burley
SHIGEZANE, Masso
SHOJI, Toshiaki
SKAGGS, Carl L.
SPEER, Herbert A.
SPRINGSTEAD, Earl R.
STUART, Amos M.
SUEOKA, Robert S.
SUNDAY, Markham R.
TABUCHI, Shigeo
TAKEUCHI, Tadash T.
THOMPSON, Kelly W.
TOKUSHIMA, Harry
TOMBLESON, Herbert
TRUJILLO, John B.
TUCKER, George D.
TURNER, Jack
TWIST, Ray E.
VOTH, Emerson
WILLIAMSON, John G.
WOLLARD, Don E.
YAMAJI, Bill Iwao
YASUDA, Joe R.
YOCKEY, William

Korean Conflict

ALBERS, Winston L. Hall, Harold L. Sr.
STUART, Herbert F. WALLACE, Carl E.

Vietnam Era

BASYE, Ralph M. McVEY, Lavoy Don
BROWN, Patrick H. MEDINA, Manuel J.
CHAVARRIA, John Marez PALACIOS, Casimiro
HARRINGTON, George M. SHIELDS, Russell
HIRSCHLER, Ralph Dean Jr. STORM, Ralph D. Jr.
LUSHER, Thomas R. VIGIL, David Lorenzo
MANLY, Frederick Lee WHITE, Donald Lee
MARQUEZ, Valentine

Thank you to Carol Grauberger, Prowers County Veterans Service Office Administrator, who provided this list for us.

ABOUT THE AUTHOR

DONNA MCDONNALL grew up listening to her brother's Army stories and her uncles' war stories. Her son, the late David McDonnall, occasionally helped translate for the military in Iraq. He and three of his companions were killed in an insurgents' attack in Mosul. To her, war is less about the politics of nations and more about the men and women representing those nations—real people with real families willing to sacrifice everything, even their own lives, so others could enjoy the comforts of freedom.

When the editor of her hometown newspaper, *The Lamar Daily News*, asked her to write a series of articles about World War II veterans in Southeast Colorado, she saw it as an opportunity to keep their stories alive.

Donna and her husband, Bruce, moved to the Wet Mountain Valley near Westcliffe, Colorado. They have two other adult children, Danny and Sara.

A registered nurse by profession, Donna also enjoys writing. She is a member of American Christian Writers and the Second Saturday Writers' Group in Westcliffe.

As a freelance writer, she has written special features and news articles for newspapers in addition to vignettes and short stories for periodicals and books. Her work has been published in *Guideposts*, *Focus on the Family*, and *Scripture Press* magazines, *Chicken Soup* books, *The Secret Place* and *Upper Room* devotionals, as well as in other magazines and books. Donna has won awards for her work at the Amarillo and the Glorieta Writers Conferences.

She hopes these stories of ordinary people from rural America who accomplished extraordinary feats will serve as a model to each of us to face our challenges with the same spirit of courage and dignity these men and women displayed.

www.ingramcontent.com/pod-product-compliance
Lightning Source LLC
Chambersburg PA
CBHW050646160426
43194CB00010B/1830